Smart Guide™
to
Maximizing Your 401(k) Plan

About Smart Guides™

Welcome to Smart Guides. Each Smart Guide is created as a written conversation with a learned friend; a skilled and knowledgeable author guides you through the basics of the subject, selecting the most important points and skipping over anything that's not essential. Along the way, you'll also find smart inside tips and strategies that distinguish this from other books on the topic.

Within each chapter you'll find a number of recurring features to help you find your way through the information and put it to work for you. Here are the user-friendly elements you'll encounter and what they mean:

The Keys
Each chapter opens by highlighting in overview style the most important concepts in the pages that follow.

Smart Money
Here's where you will learn opinions and recommendations from experts and professionals in the field.

Street Smarts
This feature presents smart ways in which people have dealt with related issues and shares their secrets for success.

Smart Sources
Each of these sidebars points the way to more and authoritative information on the topic, from organizations, corporations, government agencies, publications, web sites, and more.

Smart Definition
Terminology and key concepts essential to your mastering the subject matter are clearly explained in this feature.

F.Y.I.
Related facts, statistics, and quick points of interest are noted here.

What Matters, What Doesn't
Part of learning something new involves distinguishing the most relevant information from conventional wisdom or myth. This feature helps focus your attention on what really matters.

The Bottom Line
The conclusion to each chapter, here is where the lessons learned in each section are summarized so you can revisit the most essential information of the text.

One of the objectives of the *Smart Guide to Maximizing Your 401(k) Plan* is not only to better inform you about your 401(k) plan and the advantages of regularly investing money in it but also to make you aware that you must take charge of your financial future by planning and saving for retirement.

Smart Guide™

to

Maximizing Your 401(k) Plan

Barbara Hetzer

CADER BOOKS

John Wiley & Sons, Inc.

New York • Chichester • Weinheim • Brisbane • Singapore • Toronto

Library of Congress Cataloging-in-Publication Data:
Hetzer, Barbara.
Smart guide to maximizing your 401(k) plan / Barbara Hetzer.
p.   cm.   — (Smart guide series)
Includes index.
ISBN 0-471-35361-2 (pbk.: alk. paper)
1. 401(k) plans. 2. Individual retirement accounts. 3. Saving and
investment—United States. I. Title. II. Title: Smart guide to maximizing your four oh one (k) plan. III. Series: Smart Guides.
HD7105.45.U6H48   1999
332.024'01—dc21   99-32351

10 9 8 7 6 5 4 3 2 1

For my father,
who taught me
what it means to "maximize"

Acknowledgments

Warmest thanks to all who contributed to the research needed for this book, especially to Ted Benna, the "father" of the 401(k) plan and the president of the 401(k) Association in Bellefonte, Pennsylvania, for answering my questions—again and again; David Wray, president of the Profit Sharing/401(k) Council of America in Chicago, for his illustrative answers to my numerous questions; to Ken Alexander, of 401Komics, for his help with some pertinent charts; to Mark Mullin, Vice President and Chief Investment Officer, and to Wendy McSpedon Daniels, Vice President, of Diversified Investment Advisors in Purchase, New York, for providing so much background material; to David Godofsky, principal at Bryan, Pendleton, Swats & McAllister in Nashville, Tennessee, for his helpful charts and his willingness to "chat" on the spur of the moment; to Ed Slott, the CPA next door and his "IRA Advisor;" to Johanna Thornblad at Fidelity in Boston for compiling all that data and fielding my continual calls; to Daniel Flaherty at Fidelity for speeding along the approval process; to Deborah Liguori at PricewaterhouseCoopers in New York for her help, once again, with those hypothetical 401(k) calculations; to Jeff Close at the Spectrem Group of San Francisco for putting up with my crazy fax line; to Ed Emerman of Eagle Public Relations in New Jersey for sending that survey just when I needed it; to Tisha Findeison at Vanguard in Valley Forge, Pennsylvania; to Steven Shapiro at Scudder Kemper Investments in Boston, Massachusetts; to Jay Hoder, president of Benefit Concepts in Rhode Island; to Teresa Horney at American Association of Individual Investors in Chicago, Illinois; to Michelle Smith at the Mutual Fund Education Alliance in Kansas City, Missouri; to Patricia Curran and Holly Sheffer at the MetLife Education Center in Connecticut; to Brigid O'Connor at the Institute of Certified Financial Planners in Denver, Colorado; to Monica Gallagher and Mike Jurs at Hewitt Associates in Lincolnshire, Illinois; and to Kathy Mulvihill and Mary Anne Torswick, your "typical" retirement savers.

I'd also like to thank the *other* people who made this book possible: to John Wiley editor Debra Wishik Englander, for yet another recommendation; to Cader Books president Michael Cader, for heeding that recommendation and assigning this book to me; to Meg Drislane, who so thoroughly—yet gently—copyedited this text; and to managing editor John Jusino, for putting it all together with grace and good humor.

Contents

Introduction

Will you have enough money to retire comfortably?

That's not a trick question, but many people are genuinely stumped for an answer. Most experts say that you'll need 60 to 80 percent of your annual preretirement income to live comfortably in your golden years. But with all the talk about the eventual collapse of the Social Security system and the gradual demise of the old-fashioned "pension plan," a financially secure retirement *can* seem like the impossible dream.

If you are one of the 34 million folks nationwide who are currently contributing to a company-sponsored 401(k) plan, congratulations. You've already taken some control of your retirement future. You're smart enough to know that you can't rely on the federal government—nor your children nor anyone else—to ensure a comfortable retirement. You are responsible for building your own retirement nest egg. And contributing to a 401(k) plan is one of the easiest, and smartest, ways to do so.

Perhaps your company doesn't offer a 401(k), though, or you simply want to build additional retirement funds. Maybe, like a growing number of folks these days, you're self-employed. As a result, you may be stashing some money into an Individual Retirement Account (IRA). Again, congratulations. You've begun to take some action. Now all you need to know is how to get the most out of this type of retirement savings plan.

Whether you're currently investing in a 401(k) or an IRA—or whether you're still contemplating such an investment—the *Smart Guide to Maximizing Your 401(k) Plan* will teach you the ins and outs of retirement savings. You'll learn about eligibility, vesting, matching contributions, and other basic features of a 401(k) plan. You'll learn about deductibility, income limits, spousal contributions, and other basic features of an IRA. You'll see how an IRA stacks up against a 401(k) and how the newer Roth IRA compares to the traditional IRA.

You'll even find a primer on investing, which explains everything from stocks and bonds to the valuation of mutual funds and the use of the Standard & Poor's 500 Stock Index. You'll discover which investments are appropriate at different stages of your life. Finally, you'll learn how to withdraw your money—before retirement—if you need it, and when you must begin drawing down your account.

Best of all, you will find all of this information in a no-jargon, no-gimmick format. You'll be guided step-by-step through complicated material with understandable, commonsense advice. You'll find conventional wisdom from people who have learned by experience as well as smart tips and strategies from the experts in the field.

In chapter 1 you'll learn why—and how—you should contribute to a company-sponsored 401(k) plan. In most cases, it's hard to beat the magical effects of tax-deferred savings and any employer-matching contributions. Chapter 2 explains the key documents you'll need to review and how to make sure that your money is safe.

Don't have access to a 401(k), or want to save even more for retirement? Chapter 3 explains the basic rules of today's new and improved Individual Retirement Accounts, including the Roth IRA and the Education IRA.

To help you make sound investment decisions, chapters 4 and 5 offer a crash course in investing. You will learn about investment risk and the importance of diversification. The general asset classes—stocks, bonds, mutual funds, and cash—are explained simply and succinctly.

Where exactly should you invest those 401(k) and IRA dollars? Chapters 6 and 7 explain the investment options typically available to these retirement savings plans as well as an appropriate investment mix, based on your age, your risk tolerance, your financial goals, and other factors.

Finally, chapters 8 and 9 explain how to take the money out of your 401(k) and IRA. Whether you need the money before retirement, or sometime after, there are some restrictions concerning withdrawals.

With so many options available—not to mention all of the rules regarding contributions and withdrawals—saving for your own retirement can certainly seem overwhelming. Over time, though, you can learn enough to build a retirement nest egg. Like any other new endeavor, you must begin slowly. Bone up on the basics. Experiment a bit. Learn from your mistakes. Draw up a game plan. Review it. Revise it. Get professional advice, if necessary. And, then . . . go for it. You *can* successfully manage your 401(k) and IRA investments.

....

The 401(k): What Is It and How Does It Work?

• Automatic payroll deductions take the money out of your paycheck before you have a chance to miss it—or spend it. It's one of the easiest ways to save money.

• Pre-tax contributions to your 401(k) account mean that you keep more of your paycheck today. You'll pay taxes when you withdraw your funds at retirement, but at that point you may be in a lower tax bracket.

• Your investment earnings and dividends and capital gains reinvested in your 401(k) will grow tax-deferred until you withdraw the money from the plan. Again, at that time, you may be in a lower tax bracket.

• Take advantage of an employer match. At the very least, contribute as much to your plan as the company will match. It's free money. And the best investment return you'll find—anywhere.

Each year, two million new participants sign up for the most convenient—and often the most important—retirement savings vehicle in town. It's called a 401(k) plan, and it's offered by your employer.

Thanks to 401(k) plans, millions of working people will be able to retire comfortably. But hefty 401(k) nest eggs don't just happen. You must participate in your company's plan, and you must understand how your particular plan works, if you want to reap the rewards.

What Exactly Is a 401(k)?

A 401(k) is a type of retirement plan that is offered by your employer. It lets you save a portion of your salary for retirement. Contributions are made to the plan by you, your employer, or both of you. Any money that you contribute to such a plan is yours—even if you leave the company.

A 401(k) is often referred to as a "defined-contribution" plan. Under this arrangement, employees can "contribute" a certain amount of their salary to their accounts. They also can decide how that money is to be invested. Although investment choices are limited by the plan, most plans offer at least four different alternatives. Some plans may offer fewer selections, however, and many plans may offer eight or more.

Compare this setup to a traditional pension plan, which many people are familiar with. Unlike a 401(k), a pension plan is a "defined-benefit" plan. Under this arrangement, employers—rather than employees—contribute to the plan and they decide how the money is to be invested. A pension plan spells out in advance how much money you'll receive upon retirement. A 401(k) does not. The amount you receive upon retirement depends upon several factors, such as the size of your contribution, the size of your employer match (if any), and your investment selection. (These factors will be discussed in more detail throughout this chapter and subsequent chapters.)

Sister Plans

As popular as 401(k) plans are, not every employer offers them. Some organizations, particularly nonprofit and tax-exempt organizations, have not been allowed (under the existing tax code) to offer a 401(k) plan. Instead, these employers have offered workers a similar (but slightly different) plan called a 403(b).

Like a 401(k), a 403(b) is a retirement plan that employees contribute to that is offered by the employer. Also known as tax-sheltered annuities, 403(b)s are offered to employees who work for nonprofit or tax-exempt organizations such as schools, hospitals, or charitable foundations.

403(b)s are governed by a different section of the Internal Revenue Tax Code; hence their different name. Many aspects of these plans are similar, however, so much of the advice in this book will be applicable if you happen to have a 403(b) rather than a 401(k). Still, there are differences, so be sure to read the fine print of your company's 403(b) plan before investing any money.

An Important Tax Change

Beginning in 1997, many tax-exempt employers could begin offering 401(k) plans to their workers. Under these new pension rules, trade associations, labor organizations, and credit unions as well as tax-exempt organizations such as hospitals, research organizations, and religious or charitable institutions can now offer a 401(k) instead of a 403(b). The rules still prohibit governmental institutions—including public schools—from establishing a 401(k) plan.

Will these employers make the switch to 401(k) plans? Not necessarily. Just because an employer can now offer a 401(k) plan doesn't mean that it will. Many companies will continue to offer their already-established 403(b) programs to workers because it is often very costly to set up a new plan.

Why Contribute to Your 401(k)?

Taxes. Taxes. Taxes. One of the major attractions of a 401(k) plan is that your contributions are made with pre-tax dollars. In other words, the money that you're socking away for retirement is deducted from your paycheck before taxes are withdrawn. This means that you'll pay less in taxes right now. You won't pay any tax on the money you're contributing, in fact, until you withdraw it at retirement, which could be 20 years or more from now.

There are other advantages:

• The earnings on your investment grow tax-deferred, too, until you withdraw the money from the plan.

• Your employer may "match" the money that you contribute. Some employers match $.50 for every dollar that you contribute; others match even more. Whatever amount your employer contributes, it's free money.

• You decide how much, or how little, you want to contribute.

• Unlike with pensions and other company retirement plans, you can control (to some degree) how the money is invested in your 401(k). Most plans offer several investment choices, such as a money market account, a growth stock fund, and a bond fund, which offer varying degrees of risk.

• You can change your investment picks periodically as well as the amount that you want to contribute.

• Automatic payroll deductions make saving ultra-convenient.

• Although you pick the investments, you don't have to actually manage them yourself. Most of the choices offered are professionally managed mutual funds.

• Unlike pensions and other company retirement plans, a 401(k) is portable. If you change jobs, you can move your contributions from one

F.Y.I.

An estimated 29 million Americans at more than 320,000 companies nationwide are currently saving for retirement with a 401(k) plan. Participants have invested more than $1.5 trillion in these plans, according to the Profit Sharing/401(k) Council of America, in Chicago, Illinois.

company plan to another or you can roll your 401(k) money into a special IRA.

• Most plans allow you to withdraw your money in an emergency, such as for medical or long-term unemployment expenses, or to pay for a first home.

• Many plans allow you to borrow money from your account—and avoid taxes and penalties—if you repay the loan with interest.

• Some plans allow you to make after-tax contributions, too. You'll pay taxes on this money before you put it into your account, but you won't pay any taxes on the earnings until you withdraw it.

The Need for Your Own Retirement Savings

Still not convinced that you need the benefit of 401(k) savings? Try to think ahead to your retirement. How much money will you need to live comfortably? That depends, of course, on several factors. How old are you now and when do you hope to retire? What kind of lifestyle do you expect to enjoy during retirement?

Generally you need less income after retirement because many of your living and work-related expenses decrease. Your mortgage might be paid off by the time you retire, for instance, and you probably won't have daily commutation and lunch costs. Still, if you plan on enjoying your retirement, you'll need to replace a large portion of your salary. A common rule of thumb: Most people need about 60 percent to 80 percent of their annual pre-retirement income to live comfortably in their golden years.

Unfortunately, it's probably up to you to save and invest that money. Today's workers are increasingly on their own when it comes to building a retirement nest egg. Social Security benefits, which were never actually meant to be a person's sole means of retirement income, face an uncertain future. And traditional pension plans, which require a long career with one employer, are unrealistic for today's employee, who typically changes jobs a few times over his or her career.

That's why your 401(k) plan is such a significant benefit. A 401(k) plan lets you accumulate a substantial amount for retirement—rather easily. With its numerous tax advantages and the convenience of automatic payroll deductions, a 401(k) plan is often the best retirement savings vehicle for most people.

How a 401(k) Plan Works

401(k) plans are completely voluntary. If your employer offers such a retirement savings plan, you do not have to contribute, nor must you contribute as soon as you are eligible. You can always begin contributing money at a later date, if it's more convenient.

Contributions can be made into your account in a number of different ways:

1. The most common type of contributions are made by the employee, on a pre-tax basis, through automatic payroll deductions.

2. Some plans allow employees to make after-tax contributions.

3. Often, employers will make a matching contribution. For every dollar that you contribute, the employer will contribute $.025 to $1.00 to your account.

4. In some cases, your employer may deposit a profit-sharing contribution into your account, whether or not you sign up to make your own contributions.

If you choose to participate in a 401(k), you must decide how much money you want to put into the plan, up to certain limits defined by your company's particular plan and by the Internal Revenue Service. A percentage of your salary will then be automatically deducted from your check each pay period.

In addition, you must decide how you want to invest your savings. Do you want to put your savings into a conservative money market account? Or are you interested in a more aggressive investment, one that is better suited to your age and circumstances? Generally, you can pick from several investment options, including a variety of mutual funds. You can change your investment selection at different times during the year. And, in most cases, you can stop contributing at any time.

But First ... Eligibility Requirements

When can you join your company's plan? As soon as you're eligible. Employers can, by law, make you wait to take advantage of their 401(k) benefits. Typically, companies prohibit new participants from signing up until:

- You've worked for the company for at least one year

- You're at least 21 years old.

Employers can also exclude certain groups from participating, such as union employees and non-resident aliens. Part-timers may not be allowed to participate either. If you've just been hired recently, you may be able to sign up and begin making your own contributions immediately, but you may not be eligible for a company match until you've been with the company for six months or a year.

With a 403(b) program, however, employers have less to say about eligibility. You can often contribute from the your first day on the job if you're a full-time employee and can contribute the minimum required amount.

SMART SOURCES

Fidelity Investments is the largest provider of 401(k) plans in the country. Check out their web site, which explains the basics of a 401(k) plan. You can access the site even if your 401(k) isn't managed by Fidelity:

www.401k.com.

Making Pre-Tax Contributions

Once you're eligible to participate in your company's 401(k) plan, you must decide how much you want to contribute. One of the benefits of a 401(k), remember, is that you're saving pre-tax dollars. So . . . how much can you set aside into this account, pre-tax? That depends upon your particular plan. Contributions generally range from 2 percent to 15 percent of compensation. Each plan has a maximum contribution amount, however, which must fall within limits set by the Internal Revenue Service. In 1998, for instance, the IRS said that pre-tax contributions couldn't exceed $10,000. (This amount is adjusted annually for inflation and is sometimes referred to as the "402(g) limit.")

The amount set by the IRS represents the maximum that you can contribute, pre-tax, to all of your 401(k) accounts. It does not include any matching funds contributed by your employer. (Those contributions are counted separately.) Nor does it reduce the amount that you're allowed to contribute to other retirement plans such as an IRA.

If you work for more than one boss during the calendar year, you still have to abide by this maximum. You can't contribute more than the year's limit, even though you might have contributed to two different plans.

Automatic Payroll Deductions: The Painless Way to Save

You can't simply write a check to your 401(k) account whenever you have some extra cash on hand. The only way that you can contribute to a 401(k) plan is through an automatic payroll deduction.

Here's what happens: You tell your employer to withhold a certain percentage of your salary (called an elective deferral) each pay period. Instead of receiving your entire salary, the percentage that you "deferred" will be deposited into your 401(k) account, where that money will grow tax-deferred until you take the cash out at retirement.

Sound too disciplined? Perhaps. But the most difficult part of saving is generally finding the money at week's or month's end to set aside. Saving money via an automatic payroll deduction is convenient—and relatively painless—because your contributions go straight from your paycheck into your plan. The money is taken out of your paycheck before you have a chance to spend it.

Typically, you can sign up for inclusion in a 401(k) savings plan every quarter. Some companies offer the chance to do so every month.

If you want to increase or decrease the amount that you are currently saving—or if, in the future, you want to change the amount that you've just elected to deduct—you must call your plan administrator or human resources office to adjust your deferral percentage. (That's the percentage of your pay that you contribute to the plan).

The Pre-Tax Savings Advantage

One of the main advantages of signing up for a 401(k) or 403(b) plan is that you make your contributions to the plan with pre-tax dollars. That simply means the money you contribute to your account comes out of your paycheck before income

Contributing to Your 401(k) on a Pre-tax Basis Helps You Increase Your Take-Home Pay

	Pre-Tax Savings in Plan	Savings in a Taxable Account Outside the Plan
Annual gross salary	$50,000	$50,000
6% of pay pre-tax contribution	$ 3,000	0
Taxable pay	$47,000	$50,000
Less 28 percent federal income tax	$13,160	$14,000
6% regular savings in a taxable account outside the plan (from gross salary)	0	$ 3,000
Take-home pay	$33,840	$33,000

Annual difference in take-home pay: $840

Actual results may vary, and taxes will be due when you withdraw from the plan.

Source: Fidelity Investments. Copyright 1999 FMR Corp. All rights reserved. Reprinted by permission.

taxes are deducted. This can boost your savings in several ways:

• You pay less in taxes today. For example: Let's assume that you earned $50,000 last year and put $3,000 into your 401(k). Since your contribution was made on a pre-tax basis, your taxable income for the year was $47,000 rather than $50,000.

• Your contributions and investment earnings grow tax-deferred. You don't pay any tax on this money until you withdraw it from the plan, which ideally will be during retirement, when you might be in a lower tax bracket.

• You are investing money—and earning a return on that money—that would otherwise be paid to Uncle Sam.

Making After-Tax Contributions

Some 401(k) plans allow employees to contribute after-tax money to their accounts as well. An after-tax contribution comes out of your pay *after* taxes have been deducted. This kind of contribution does not reduce your taxable income. The earnings grow tax-deferred, though—just like the earnings on pre-tax contributions—until you withdraw the money. Some employers match after-tax contributions, but the majority of employers match just pre-tax contributions.

If you are not contributing the maximum allowed by your plan, however, you shouldn't even consider this option. Your first goal should always be to max out on your pre-tax 401(k) contributions.

Who should take advantage of this option, then? Employees who aren't permitted to contribute the legal limit of pre-tax contributions set by the Internal Revenue Service because the government deems that they are too "highly compensated."

Huh? When 401(k) plans came to be, the IRS was concerned that these plans might unfairly favor highly paid employees. So they devised a test, called the "nondiscrimination" test, which says basically that if you earn too much money (in 1988, that meant more than $80,000), your pre-tax contributions might be limited because you rank as a "highly compensated" employee.

If you fall into this category, you may be limited to contribute a certain percentage of your salary—which is far less than the $10,000 pre-tax maximum contribution allowed by law. It is at this point, then, that you might want to consider making after-tax contributions to your 401(k). Although you must pay tax on this money now, the earnings on your contributions will still grow tax-deferred.

Pre-Tax Contributions versus After-Tax Contributions

Some 401(k) plans permit both pre-tax and after-tax contributions. Generally, pre-tax contributions are your best bet for the reasons discussed above. After-tax contributions can be advantageous, though, in certain situations.

Pre-Tax Contributions ...

• Come out of your pay before taxes are deducted.

• Lower your current taxable income.

• Are taxed as ordinary income when you withdraw the money from the plan.

• May be withdrawn from the plan before age 59½ only if you have a qualified financial hardship. (Otherwise, you'll incur a 10 percent penalty and income tax on the withdrawn amount.)

After-Tax Contributions ...

• Come out of your pay after taxes have been deducted.

• Don't lower your current taxable income.

• Are not taxed at withdrawal because you've already paid taxes on the money. (You do have to pay tax on any investment earnings.)

• May be withdrawn from most plans for any reason. (You'll have to pay income tax on your investment earnings only—not on the contributions.)

The Tax-Deferred Investment Earnings Advantage

Another advantage of saving in a 401(k) or 403(b) plan is that investment earnings and dividends and capital gains reinvested in your company's plan will not be taxed—until you withdraw the money from the plan. All withdrawals will be taxed as ordinary income at this point, but ideally you won't be withdrawing the money until retirement, when you might be in a lower tax bracket. If you withdraw your funds early (that's before age 59½), you may owe a 10 percent early-withdrawal penalty in addition to the ordinary income taxes due.

Of course, in addition to accumulating on a tax-deferred basis, your 401(k) investments also benefit from the power of compounding. This means that every year your account will grow by the amount that you contribute *plus* the earnings from the previous years.

Saving on a tax-deferred basis can increase your investment returns. Over time, a tax-deferred nest egg can grow significantly larger than an equivalent taxable investment because more money stays in your account, and keeps growing.

For example: If you contributed some $2,000 per year into your 401(k) and your account earned 8 percent a year for 30 years, you would have $260,000. That would be $100,000 more than if your annual investment went into an ordinary taxable account.

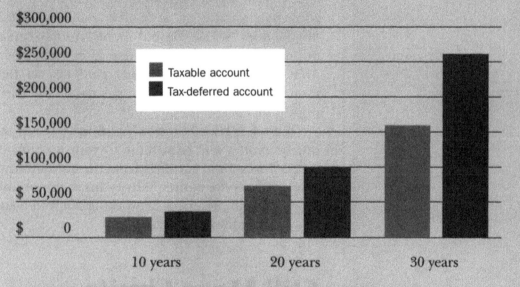

Benefits of Tax-Deferred Investing in a 401(k) Plan

This chart compares the rate of return over 30 years for a taxable account and a tax-deferred account. (Assumes 8% annual return and 25% combined state and federal tax bracket.) Earnings will vary according to your own tax bracket and annual rate of return.

- Taxable account
- Tax-deferred account

Source: 401Komics, product of the 401(k) Association. (Chart for illustrative purposes only.)

More than a Mutual Fund

Why not simply save money in your own mutual fund or bank account rather than contributing to a 401(k)? Because you'll lose out on the tax-savings advantages that a 401(k) offers. An ordinary mutual fund or savings account, for example, doesn't allow you to save on a tax-deferred basis like a 401(k) does. When you put money into a regular mutual fund, you're investing after-tax dollars. That means you have already paid tax on that money. In addition, you must pay tax on the earnings of that account every year.

With a 401(k), however, you don't pay any tax on the money you contribute to your account or on the investment earnings from the account until you withdraw the money. Why is this so important? More of your paycheck is working for you—and less is going toward taxes.

Still More Limits

The IRS isn't happy just limiting the amount that highly paid workers can contribute to their 401(k)s. The government also imposes limits on the total amount that can be contributed to your 401(k) account in a given year. These limits, which are found in Section 415 of the Internal Revenue Tax Code, say that all contributions—made by you and/or your employer—may not exceed 25 percent of the employee's salary, or $30,000. This cap includes your pre-tax and after-tax contributions, your employer's match, and your employer's profit-sharing contributions.

Why does the government care how much you contribute to a 401(k)? Because they want to keep that tax revenue stream rolling. Uncle Sam doesn't receive any federal taxes on the money you defer into your 401(k). (The government will receive tax payment later, when you withdraw the money from your account.) By limiting the amount of money that you can defer into your 401(k), the government is basically ensuring that you'll still owe them at least some money for federal taxes on the remainder of your paycheck today.

The Employer Match

Some employers "match" a portion of what employees save in a 401(k). That means for every dollar that you contribute, your employer will kick in some money, too. A match typically ranges from $.25 to $1.00, but the most common match is $.50 for every dollar you contribute, up to 6 percent of pay.

To qualify for a match, your plan may require that you work for the company a certain number of years and/or that you contribute a certain amount to your 401(k) (3 percent of your salary, for instance).

At the very least, you should contribute as much as the company will match. Otherwise, you'll be throwing free money away. And with these bonus bucks, your retirement nest egg will grow that much faster.

For example: Jane participates in her 401(k) plan. She usually puts 5 percent of her $50,000

STREET SMARTS

"Every time I get a raise I increase my contribution. It's an easy way to save because I never see that money. And those extra dollars would just get spent on little things," says Kathryn Mulvihill, a 38-year-old accountant who has been contributing to her company's 401(k) plan since 1990.

Employer Matching Contributions

Nine out of 10 plans match before-tax employee contributions. Two-thirds of plans (57 percent) provide a fixed match on employee contributions. The most common type of fixed employer matching contribution is $.50 per $1.00, up to a specified percent of pay.

Type of Employer Match	Percent of Plans
Fixed match (e.g., $.50 per $1.00 up to 6% of pay)	67%
Graded match (e.g., $1.00 per $1.00 on first 3%; $.50 per $1.00 on next 3%)	14%
Match based on company performance	14%
Match based on length of employee's service	6%
Other match (e.g., age-based match, capped matches)	10%
No employer match	7%

Source: 401(k) Trends and Experience; Hewitt Associates, Lincolnshire, Illinois, 1997.

salary into the plan. Her company has begun offering a $.50 match for every dollar that Jane contributes, up to 6 percent. To take full advantage of the match, Jane has decided to increase her contribution this year to 6 percent. As a result, Jane will contribute $3,000 this year. Her employer will contribute $1,500. That's a 50 percent return on her money—and Jane hasn't even invested it yet.

Jane's 6% Contribution	$3,000
Her Employer's Match	$1,500
Jane's Total Contribution	$4,500

Are You Vested?

Your 401(k) plan is portable. If you leave your job, get fired or laid off, or take early retirement, you can take your 401(k) plan with you. You can move your contributions from one company plan to another, or you can roll your 401(k) money into a special IRA.

The money that you have contributed from your paycheck through automatic payroll deductions, as well as the earnings on those contributions, is yours—no matter how long or how briefly you've been contributing to the plan. That's not necessarily so with your employer's matching contributions, however.

How much of those contributions you keep will depend upon your company's "vesting" schedule. Vesting schedules differ from one company to another, so you'll have to check with your employer to find out the exact rules of your plan. Under a typical vesting schedule, however, your rights to matching contributions increase with the number of years that you've been on the job. After a certain time period (but no longer than seven years, usually), you are generally considered "fully vested." At that time, you can take all your 401(k) contributions—including your company's matching contributions—with you should you leave the company.

Some employers give immediate vesting, but

most employers adhere to one of the following vesting schedules:

• **Cliff Vesting.** Under these guidelines, you aren't vested until a certain time period has elapsed. If you leave your job before that time, you get none of your employer's contributions. If you leave after that time, you get to keep all of your employer's contributions.

• **Graded Vesting.** Under these guidelines, you gradually earn the right to keep a percentage of your employer's contributions with every year that you are employed by the company. After three years, for instance, you may be vested in 25 percent of employer contributions. By year seven, you should be 100 percent vested. If you leave after this point, you get to keep all of the money.

What You Lose If You Leave Before Vesting

Your decision to leave an employer before your employer's 401(k) contributions are fully vested may not be an easy one. You'll have to weigh certain factors, including, of course, the importance of a career move at this time.

Here's what you stand to lose financially if you leave your job before you're fully vested:

Let's assume that your employer offers the most common type of matching contribution: The company will match $.50 for every $1.00 that you contribute, up to 6 percent of your salary. You earn $60,000 per year, and you contribute 6 percent of your salary annually. That means you contribute $3,600 to your 401(k) each year; your employer contributes $1,800.

After four years, your employer will have contributed $7,200. If your company employs a five-year cliff vesting schedule, you won't get to keep a penny of that $7,200 because you are leaving the company before you are fully vested.

Your Employer's Profit-Sharing Contribution

Your company may not offer matching contributions. Instead, it may contribute a fixed percentage of each eligible employee's salary to his or her account—whether or not the employee signs up to make his or her own contributions. The amount of this contribution, which is generally referred to as a profit-sharing contribution, is often based on the company's profitability that year. Like the matching contribution, this is free money. But, in this instance, you don't even have to contribute any money to reap the benefits. Here's how this employer contribution works:

Joe's employer offers a 401(k) plan. The plan does not match employee contributions. Instead, Joe's employer offers a profit-sharing contribution. The company contributes 2 percent of each eligible employee's salary to his or her retirement account.

Last year Joe earned $50,000. He did not defer any of his income, however, into his 401(k). Still, a

WHAT MATTERS, WHAT DOESN'T

What Matters
• Contribute early, and often.

• Take advantage of pre-tax contributions. You'll pay less in taxes now, thereby giving you more money to invest.

• Understand the rules. How much do you have to contribute to receive your company's full matching contribution, for instance? When do you become vested?

What Doesn't
• Can't afford to take the maximum contribution? Don't let that prevent you from contributing. Start small and increase the amount over time.

• Plan on switching jobs in the near future? Not to worry. Your 401(k) contributions go with you. You may lose your employer's matching contributions, though, depending on the vesting schedule.

contribution of $1,000 (that's 2 percent of $50,000) was made to his plan by his employer.

Not Your Typical Profit-Sharing Plan

A profit-sharing plan is a type of retirement plan that some companies offer to their employees. Under this arrangement, the company "shares" its annual profits with employees by contributing, at year's end, a percentage of the company's profits to each worker's account. In a profitable year, a company may contribute generously (up to certain limits). In a bad year, the company may elect not to make any contributions for that particular year at all.

You do not contribute to a profit-sharing plan—unless your company's profit-sharing plan has a 401(k) component. A 401(k) is actually just part of a profit-sharing plan. In this case, employers may continue to contribute a fixed amount or percentage of the company's profits into employee's accounts each year. But the added twist with a 401(k) plan is that employees can make additional contributions—with pre-tax dollars. Current income taxes are deferred on both employer and employee contributions and on all investment earnings until you take the money out of the plan. Employers can also contribute additional monies into employees' accounts in the form of matching contributions.

Those Contributions Really Add Up

There's a more in-depth discussion of how much money you can save with a 401(k) through compounding and a long time horizon in chapter 4. But for a quick idea of just how powerful an investment tool a 401(k) plan can be, consider the following:

Bill's 401(k) Contributions Over Time

Bill earns $65,000 per year. He has just begun participating in his company's 401(k) plan and has elected to save 10 percent of his salary. (That's $6,500 this year.) His employer offers a $0.50 match on the first 6 percent, which boosts his contribution by another $1,950 this year to $8,450. Every year thereafter, Bill receives a 4.5 percent salary increase. He continues to put a full 10 percent of his salary into his 401(k) and his company continues to offer a $0.50 match on the first 6 percent. Assuming that he receives an average return of 8 percent on his savings, Bill will have stockpiled $303,693 in just 15 years.

Year	Employee Contribution	50% Employer Match on First 6%	Earnings	Year-End Balance
1	$ 6,500	$1,950	$ 317	$ 8,767
5	$ 7,751	$2,325	$ 3,885	$ 56,215
10	$ 9,660	$2,898	$11,260	$153,806
15	$10,000	$3,000	$21,557	$303,693

Source: PricewaterhouseCoopers LLP Personal Financial Services, New York, New York.

As you can see, it really does pay to start saving often, and early. The sooner you start saving, the longer your money has to grow. That means you'll have to save less to meet your financial goals if you start early. What's more, if your employer matches your contributions, you can earn up to a 100 percent return on your money before you even invest it. All of these advantages make 401(k) plans one of the best retirement savings deals around.

THE BOTTOM LINE

A 401(k) plan is an easy way for many people to save for retirement—and it's just sitting at your employer's doorstep. These plans offer numerous tax advantages.

Unlike traditional pension plans, you have some control over how your savings are invested in a 401(k) plan. Plus, many plans let you withdraw funds in an emergency or borrow against your account. Best of all, your 401(k) is portable. If you quit your job or get fired or laid off, you can take the money with you.

....

CHAPTER 2

Under-standing the Fine Print

THE KEYS

• The responsibility for managing your 401(k) account is shared among various "players," such as the plan sponsor, the administrator, and the investment manager.

• Most employers offer a 401(k) plan to their employees because it is a way to recruit and retain valuable workers.

• It's probably unlikely that your company will misuse your 401(k) contributions. But you should review your account statement periodically to ensure your money is safe.

• Your 401(k) money is safe from creditors, but not necessarily from a spouse in the case of divorce.

Whether you have just decided to join your company's 401(k) plan or you want to learn how to take better advantage of the 401(k) plan that you are already contributing to, you should spend a few moments reading the fine print of your plan's enrollment package. Too often, participants—even longtime participants—simply shelve this material for future reference without ever actually reviewing it. And that can be a costly mistake in the long run with regard to retirement plans.

If you expect to make the most of your 401(k) plan, however, you should understand your employer's (and your) responsibilities and obligations in regard to the plan. How can you tell if the folks entrusted with your 401(k) contributions are handling your money properly, for instance? Who is responsible if the investments in your account decline in value? The documentation that your employer is required to supply should answer most of these questions.

To find out exactly what your company's plan provides, read all the materials provided and check out the fine print.

Key Documents

Your employer will provide you with some information about the investment options available through your 401(k) plan. These documents, which can include a summary plan description, a prospectus, and/or a fact sheet, will outline each investment's potential risks and rewards.

The Summary Plan Description

When you enroll in your company plan, you'll receive a booklet called the Summary Plan Description. (Some companies may give it another title, but it serves the same function.) This booklet, which describes your company's 401(k) plan in some detail, is generally quite lengthy. A copy should be given to you no more than 90 days after you become a participant, and you should also get an updated version of this document every five years. Many employees don't take the time to read this document, but you should. It explains all of your 401(k)'s features, including:

- Eligibility to participate

- Vesting

- How the company match is calculated

- Death benefits for beneficiaries

- Loans

In addition, the Summary Plan Description explains your legal rights and gives the name and address of your plan administrator and trustee. The Summary Plan Description is simply a summary of the Plan Document, a more detailed account of how your 401(k) works. The Summary Plan Description is written in simple language and is generally much easier to understand than the Plan Document itself.

The Summary Plan Description

The Summary Plan Description, or SPD, explains how your 401(k) plan works. It provides a "summary" of your benefits and rights under your particular plan. Most are written in a reader-friendly style, as the following excerpts from a generic plan drafted by Diversified Investment Advisors in Purchase, New York, suggest:

Vesting

Vesting means ownership of your account. It is the part of your account that is yours.

Maximum Annual Contributions

The most that may be contributed to your account is the lesser of $30,000 or 25 percent of your total salary.

Tax Advantages

You don't have to pay taxes on contributions and earnings until you withdraw them from the plan.

Your Contributions

You may contribute between 1 percent and 15 percent of your salary.

Prospectus and/or Fact Sheet

If you invest in a mutual fund, you should receive a prospectus listing the stocks or bonds in which the mutual fund invests as well as the rules governing the fund and a profile of the investment managers. Fact sheets, on the other hand, typically explain what each investment is and how it works. For instance, a fact sheet may explain the potential risks of a particular type of investment and provide some background as to how this type of investment has performed in the past and in comparison to other investments.

Individual Account Statement

Your employer is required to tell you how your 401(k) account is doing. Your account statement will tell you how much money you have accrued in total (including vested benefits) up to this time; where your money is currently invested; and if you've borrowed or withdrawn any funds from your account. Your employer, or your plan's provider, must send you an account statement at least once per year, but many send quarterly account statements.

Key Players in Your 401(k) Plan

Every 401(k) involves a number of "players" who are responsible for managing certain aspects of

SMART DEFINITION

Plan provider

A plan provider is an outside partner that's running your company's 401(k) plan. In some cases, the plan provider could "provide" nearly all of the tasks needed, including administration, record keeping, and investment management.

your plan. Plans vary, of course. Some plans have one provider who basically "bundles" all or most of the services offered below. (The one exception: The plan sponsor is always your company.) Others outsource the various services to different players:

Plan Sponsor

Your employer, who offers the 401(k) plan to you as an employee of the company, is the plan sponsor. Your employer makes decisions regarding your plan, including the investment choices that will be offered to you.

Plan Trustee

Your employer is required by law to act on your behalf to protect your interests. (This is sometimes referred to as a "fiduciary" responsibility.) Companies, therefore, will often appoint an outside firm (called a trustee or a custodian) to monitor the administration of the company's 401(k) plan. Generally, the trustee is a bank or an investment firm, though the trustee could also be a few individuals from the company itself. It is the trustee's job to act as the guardian of the money. For instance, the trustee will make sure that your money is invested properly and that all regulations and rules are followed. Generally, the trustee has no authority as to how that money is invested, however.

Plan Administrator

The plan administrator manages the daily activities of your company's 401(k) plan. For instance, the plan administrator will file the necessary reports and tax forms and handle loans, withdrawals, and payroll deductions. It is also the plan administrator's job to answer employees' questions about the plan. In many cases, the plan administrator will deal with employees through personnel or the human resources department.

Record Keeper

The record keeper tracks your account's activity:

- How much money you contribute

- How much money you withdraw

- The investments that you have chosen

The record keeper will send you an account statement—usually every quarter—that states all of the above information as well as how much your account is currently worth. Many employers hire a professional record keeping company to do this work for them. In some companies, the record keeper may also be the investment manager.

Investment Manager

One of the advantages of a 401(k) is that you can often pick from several investment choices. Those investment choices are offered to you by a professional money management firm, which buys and sells investments for you. The money management firm is hired by your employer.

Need Help? Your Employer Can Explain

Understanding the intricacies of your particular 401(k) plan can be tricky. But helpful information may be at your fingertips. Over half of the employers surveyed by Hewitt Associates, a benefits consulting firm in Lincolnshire, Illinois, in their 1997 survey, say that they provide formal investment education aimed at making employees more knowledgeable about retirement planning.

What kind of help can you expect?

• **Seminars and Workshops.** This is one of the most popular medium used to get the 401(k) word out. Almost all of the companies that offer such workshops, according to the Hewitt study, say that they're effective.

• **One-on-One Counseling.** Less than half of the companies use this method.

• **Written Materials.** Every company provides employees with some literature explaining their 401(k) plan. Some also offer video or audio materials as well.

• **Internet Access.** A growing number of companies are now posting their 401(k) information on a web site. Often these sites will include a "calcula-tor," which can help you figure out how much you need to save for retirement.

401(k) Fees

It costs money to run a 401(k) plan. And, in many cases, your employer may be passing these costs on to you. You should understand what charges you're paying because substantial fees can impact your savings growth.

Plan Adminstration Fees

All 401(k) plans offer basic administrative services, such as plan record keeping, accounting, and legal and trustee services. In addition, many plans now offer other services as well, such as retirement planning software, online transactions, and invest-ment advice.

Basic administrative services may be covered by investment fees (see "Investment Fees" below), but administrative fees may also be charged separately. Your employer may pick up the tab, or you, the participant, may bear the cost.

There are two ways participants pay adminis-tration fees. You may pay a flat fee or you may pay a percentage of your account balance. (In the lat-ter case, then, participants with larger account bal-ances pay more, for instance, than those with smaller account balances.)

SMART SOURCES

To find out about 401(k) fees, check out:

• A fund's prospectus, which describes the fees associated with your investment

• Your account state-ment, which may show administrative expenses charged to your account

• The Summary Plan Description, which may tell you if administra-tive expenses are paid by your plan—rather than by your employer—and how those expenses are allocated among plan participants

• The plan's annual report, which shows the total administrative fees and other expenses paid by the plan. It will not show expenses deducted from investment results, however, or fees and expenses paid by your individual account. Fees paid by your employer will not be shown either.

SMART SOURCES

For additional information about fees typically charged to 401(k) plans, check out the Pension and Welfare Benefits Admistration's Study of 401(k) Plan Fees and Expenses. Contact them at:

Pension and Welfare
 Benefits Administration
U.S. Department of
 Labor
Room N-5625
200 Constitution
 Avenue, N.W.
Washington, D.C.
 20210
800-998-7542
www.dol.gov/dol/pwba

Investment Fees

You may also be charged fees related to the different investments offered through your plan. Called investment fees, these are generally assessed as a percentage of assets invested. You may not even be aware that you're paying investment fees, however, because they're not charged to you directly.

In nearly all cases, these fees are deducted from your investment returns before your return is calculated. That means your total investment return is your return *after* these fees have been deducted. You can easily overlook these charges because they are generally not identified on account statements. You have to read your fund's prospectus to find out what charges are levied.

Some common investment fees include:

Sales Charges

Some mutual funds levy a sales charge (commonly referred to as a load) when you buy or sell shares in the fund. A fee that is charged when you buy shares is called a front load. A fee that is charged when you sell shares is called a back load. A front load is deducted from your initial investment. A back load may decrease and eventually be eliminated over time.

Some mutual funds don't charge any fees for buying or selling shares. This is called a no-load fund. Some no-load funds charge an annual operating fee, however, called a 12b-1 fee. This should be a small amount (between 0.25 percent and 1 percent of annual assets), but it sometimes is not. A 12b-1 fee is used to pay for marketing and advertising expenses.

Management Fees

Also called investment advisory fees or account maintenance fees, these are ongoing charges for managing the investment fund's assets. Generally, they are a percentage of the assets invested in the fund, but they can vary widely from one plan to another. A guaranteed investment contract fund generally charges some management and administrative fees.

How Does Your Company's Plan Rate?

The Employee Retirement Income Security Act (commonly referred to as ERISA) determines how 401(k)s operate. This federal law tells companies what they can and cannot do. That doesn't mean that all 401(k)s are exactly alike—as you now know, all 401(k) plans aren't alike. Your specific 401(k) plan was created by your employer. It may contain certain features, such as a matching contribution, that other plans do not. It all depends on what your employer has decided to include. Compare its features to the typical 401(k) plan (see pages 38–39) and test the desirability of your company's 401(k). Consider the following:

• Does your employer offer a matching contribution? If your employer is making contributions on your behalf (based on a certain percentage that you contribute), you'll be throwing those employer contributions away if you don't sign up. Of course, if your employer makes those contributions whether

The Typical 401(k) Plan

		Most Frequent Response, 1998
Level of Participation	The average participation rate is 77%.	
Eligibility	Plan participants are typically enrolled after a 12-month waiting period.	52%
Employee Contributions	Nearly two-thirds of the plans have one maximum contribution limit for all employees.	65%
	The most common pre-tax contribution permitted is 15% of salary (for plans with one maximum).	52%
	Two-thirds of the plans do not allow post-tax contributions.	67%
Employer Matching Contributions	The vast majority of the plans provide matching contributions.	89%
	The most prevalent matching formula is a fixed amount per dollar up to a maximum percentage of salary.	61%
	The most common employer match amount is $.50 per dollar.	49%
	The most common percentage of pay matched is 6%.	46%
	Employer matching contributions are typically made with cash.	84%

Investments	Plans typically have 6 to 9 investment options	89%
	Employees are typically permitted to change investment elections for future contributions every pay period.	70%
	Employees are typically permitted to change investment elections for existing account balances daily.	71%
Loans & Withdrawals	The typical plan has a loan provision.	87%
	Plan sponsors generally charge participants a fee for taking a loan.	70%
	The typical minimum loan amount is $1,000.	75%
	Prime rate +1% is the most common rate used to set the loan interest rate.	48%
	Hardship withdrawals are the most common type of in-service withdrawals permitted.	92%
Record Keeping & Administration	Plan sponsors typically use voice response systems to communicate account balance information.	85%
	Plan valuations are typically processed on a daily basis.	72%
	Plan sponsors typically reported that their plan is in compliance with ERISA 404(c).	84%

Source: Buck Consultants, *401(k) Plans: Survey Report on Plan Design,* 1998.

or not you contribute, well, there is no decision to make. You're being handed money, and you don't even need to participate.

• How many investment options can you choose from? 401(k) plans often offer various investment options, including stock, bond, and money market mutual funds. But more options doesn't necessarily mean you'll have better options. The key question: Does your 401(k) offer an investment (or a few investments) that fit your long-term financial goals and your investment risk tolerance? (For a more detailed discussion of investment risk and financial goals, see chapter 4.)

• How accessible is the plan? A 401(k) plan will be more attractive to you, a new participant, if you can enroll soon after starting employment; if you can roll over money from your former employer's 401(k) account into your new one; and if your company runs workshops and has literature explaining the rules.

Why Companies Offer 401(k)s

401(k)s cost employers money to fund and operate. Yet more and more companies now offer such plans, and increasingly more employees are taking advantage of such plans. How come?

• It's a dog-eat-dog world out there. Companies must remain competitive. Employers hope that by offering a 401(k) plan and other attractive benefits, they'll be able to recruit and retain valuable employees.

• Most employers realize that workers are responsible for securing their own retirement funds. This is their way of helping you reach those goals.

• A 401(k) is cheaper for an employer to fund than a traditional pension plan because the company doesn't have to contribute all of the money itself. You, the employee, contribute money from your own paycheck.

Is Your Money Safe?

401(k) plans are subject to comprehensive regulations enforced by the Internal Revenue Service, the Department of Labor, and the Securities and Exchange Commission.

Yet a few years back, stories surfaced about how some companies had improperly used their employees' 401(k) funds. Some of these firms were accused of using their employees' 401(k) contributions to cover the company's operating expenses. Other companies were accused of stealing the funds and using the money to pay for private expenses.

Could this happen today? Of course. The truth is, though, that most investors have no reason to be concerned about the safety of their 401(k) plans. The contributions made to a 401(k) are held in trust. The trustee is responsible for investing your money and making sure that the plan complies with government regulations. Legally, your employer can't touch your money.

But what about those cases where employers clearly *did* dip into their employees' accounts? The misuse of those funds occurred at a very small number of companies. And the companies in question were also very small in size. The likelihood that your employer would steal your 401(k) funds are slim.

Held in Trust

The money that you plunk into a 401(k) is protected by the Employee Retirement Income Security Act (ERISA) of 1974, which says basically that each company's 401(k) plan assets must be managed according to established guidelines. The money in your 401(k) plan—that includes your contributions and all vested company contributions—is held in trust in a separate account (for you) by your employer. It is not mixed with the company's other assets. Only you have access to that money. That means the company cannot use that retirement fund money for its business. So even if your employer went bankrupt, your retirement money would still be untouched (and safe) in its own separate account.

Each plan has a group of players (discussed in "Key Players in Your 401(k) Plan," page 31), who provide a sort of checks-and-balance system. The trustee, for example, is responsible for collecting money and investing it. The record keeper is responsible for keeping track of employees' contributions. And the investment manager is responsible for buying and selling those investments for you.

No Federal Guarantees

That said, however, there is no federal agency safe-guarding your money. Unlike the money you put into a bank account, which is insured up to $100,000 by the federal government, and unlike the benefits from a traditional pension plan, which are insured by the Pension Benefit Guaranty Corporation, the money in your 401(k) is not guaranteed by anyone.

Your employer is legally responsible, of course, for offering good investment choices and for keeping your contributions safe from creditors or from anyone intending to use that money for company business. But you are ultimately responsible for picking—and monitoring—your investments. Choose wisely from among the offered alternatives, and you'll build a sizable nest egg. Choose poorly, and you could lose some money.

How much your 401(k) account will be worth in the future depends on:

- How much money you contribute

- How much money your employer contributes (if anything)

- How the investments that you select perform over time

404(c) Regulations

To protect itself from liability due to losses associated with 401(k) plans, your company may comply with the 404(c) regulations set by the Department

SMART MONEY

Is my 401(k) account at risk if my employer goes out of business?

"No," says Ted Benna, the "father" of the 401(k) plan and president of the 401(k) Association in Bellefonte, Pennsylvania. "Your account is protected if your company goes out of business. The plan sponsor is required to deposit 401(k) contributions into a separate trust account within a reasonable period after they've been deducted from your paycheck. The trust is a separate legal entity from your employer. The company's creditors have no claim, legally, to 401(k) funds."

WHAT MATTERS, WHAT DOESN'T

What Matters

• Read your summary plan description. It explains how your 401(k) plan works.

• Review your account statement periodically.

What Doesn't

• Don't worry unneccesarily about your plan's safety. Most 401(k) plans are well managed.

• Your 401(k) plan doesn't offer as many options as your best friend's plan. It's probably still worthwhile to contribute. It's hard to beat the tax-deferred savings advantage of a 401(k).

of Labor. (These regulations come from section 404(c) of ERISA, the federal law that sets the minimum standards for 401(k)s and other pension plans.) Many companies now meet these standards (or are trying to), which say that you, the 401(k) plan participant, must be given:

• At least three different investment choices, which offer varying levels of risk

• Enough information to make "informed" decisions about those investments

• The opportunity to move your money—and change the amount that you're investing—among those investment choices at least every three months

A Few Other Rules to Note

Employers must comply with a few procedural rules for 401(k)s, however. First, a 401(k) can't discriminate in favor of top-salaried employees. In other words, rank-and-file employees must be allowed the same benefits as those who are more highly compensated. Second, your company can't prevent you from participating in the plan (if you meet eligibility rules). And, finally, your employer can't prevent you from taking your retirement money with you when you leave the company.

Some Red Flags

While you shouldn't worry unnecessarily about the security of your 401(k) funds, it's smart to keep a watchful eye for unexplained discrepancies, such as the following:

• You haven't received an account statement, detailing your contributions. Or it's been at least six months since you received your last statement.

• You have yet to receive a Summary Plan Description or a Plan Document—even though you've asked for these documents at least two or three times.

• There is no record of your employer's matching contribution on your account statement. (And you are contributing enough to take advantage of your employer's match.)

• Your investments have been reallocated—without your consent.

• The amount that you believe you have contributed to your account is not reflected on your account statement.

Special Circumstances

Your 401(k) is protected should your employer go bankrupt. But what if you declare personal bankruptcy or get divorced? What if you die? Can someone else lay claim to your retirement nest egg?

If You Declare Personal Bankruptcy

You may lose your home, your car, and your base-ball card collection, but you won't lose your 401(k) benefits in personal bankrupcy. Federal law prohibits creditors from forcing you to liquidate your account to pay the debts owed them.

If You Get Divorced

In the case of a divorce, your spouse, child, or other dependent can claim a share of your 401(k) benefits. A court may issue what's known as a Qualified Domestic Relations Order (the abbreviation QDRO is pronounced *quadro*). This court order awards a specified amount or percentage of your 401(k) benefits as payment of alimony, child support, or the division of property.

Your spouse may be able to leave his or her share of your 401(k) in the plan. (This depends on what the court order says and what your 401(k) plan permits.) If your spouse takes his or her share out of the plan, however, he or she must pay income tax on those withdrawals. But under a QDRO, your spouse does not have to pay that 10 percent early-withdrawal penalty, even if he or she is younger than age 59½.

If You Die

When you die, your spouse is generally assumed to be the beneficiary of your 401(k) plan, unless you have specified otherwise. You can name someone else as the beneficiary on your account—such as your brother or children—but if you're married, you must get your spouse's consent in writing to do so.

If your spouse is the beneficiary, he or she can roll the account over into a special Individual Retirement Account (IRA), or withdraw the money as a lump sum. (For a fuller discussion of an IRA rollover, see chapter 7.) As with a QDRO, if he or she withdraws the money, he or she must pay income tax on that withdrawal. However, he or she does not have to pay the 10 percent early-withdrawal penalty, even if he or she is younger than age 59½.

THE BOTTOM LINE

Your 401(k) is your best ticket to a secure retirement. Make sure that you receive—and review—all the available documentation about the rules and requirements of your plan as well as the fees charged. Ask your employer or the plan provider if any investment education program, such as a retirement planning seminar or a videotape, is available.

....

The IRA: What Is It and How Does It Work?

What's that? You are self-employed and, thus, don't have access to a 401(k) plan? Or, your employer doesn't offer one? If you've been on the job for a while, you may want to consider approaching your boss or human resources department about starting up such a plan. (Be sure to mention what a powerful employee retention tool a 401(k) plan is.) In the meantime, consider saving for your retirement with an Individual Retirement Account (commonly known as an IRA). Self-employed folks can set up a special IRA, called a Simplified Employee Pension (SEP), or SEP-IRA.

Even if your employer does offer a 401(k) (or some other type of retirement savings plan), you may still want to think about an IRA if you'd like to stash supplemental retirement savings. You now have several smart choices to pick from: the traditional IRA (deductible and nondeductible varieties); the new tax-free Roth IRA; and the new Education IRA, which isn't really a retirement savings vehicle at all.

What Exactly Is an IRA?

An Individual Retirement Account (IRA) is a personal savings plan that lets you put aside money for your retirement or, in some plans, for certain education expenses. Unlike a 401(k) plan, an IRA is not offered by your employer. It is a retirement savings account that you set up yourself at a bank, a mutual fund company, or through your stockbroker. Funds in an IRA may be invested in a variety of vehicles, including stocks and bonds.

Each year, you can contribute up to $2,000 to your IRA account. (Contributions to an Education IRA are limited to $500 per year, however.) You can plunk $2,000 into your IRA *every year,* as long as you meet the following two criteria:

1. You must have earned income, or compensation, for the year that you put money into the IRA.

2. You must be under age 70½.

If you're over age 70½, you can still keep your IRA account. You just can't open a new IRA account or continue to make annual contributions to an account that you already have.

In return for your investment, you may receive the following tax advantages:

• **Tax Deductions.** You may be able to deduct all, or a portion, of your IRA contributions from your gross income. It depends on the type of IRA used and if you meet certain eligibility requirements.

For instance: If you do not have a retirement savings plan through your employer, you can probably deduct your full annual contribution to a traditional IRA on your tax return.

• **Tax Savings.** Money contributed to your IRA—including earnings and gains on those contributions—is not taxed until you take the money out at retirement. In some cases, the money may not be taxed at all.

Generally, money taken out of an IRA before age 59½ is subject to a 10 percent early-withdrawal

SMART DEFINITION

Compensation

Generally, what you earn from working is compensation. That includes wages, salaries, tips, professional fees, bonuses, and commissions that you receive for providing personal services. Also included, according to the IRS, is taxable alimony payments that you receive under a divorce decree. What's not included? Income that you receive from a rental property, for instance, and interest and dividend income received from any investments.

penalty and ordinary income taxes. In addition, you generally can't borrow money from your IRA, but withdrawals are permitted (before age 59½) to pay for certain expenses, such as a first-time home purchase and some medical and long-term unemployment expenses, without incurring a 10 percent early-withdrawal penalty.

A Brief History of the IRA

1974: The IRA Is Introduced
The Individual Retirement Account, created as part of the Employee Retirement Income Security Act of 1974, is a convenient way for Americans who don't have pension or retirement plans to save for their own retirement. Individuals who meet the eligibility requirements can make tax-deductible contributions, and earnings grow tax-deferred.

1982: Everyone Jumps On the IRA Bandwagon
Thanks to President Ronald Reagan's Economic Recovery Tax Act of 1981, the IRA is suddenly a very popular way for folks to save. Why? Eligibility standards have been loosened. Prior to 1982, only workers who had no pension or retirement plan through their employers could open an IRA. Now, under Reagan's new tax bill, virtually anyone who earns an income can open an IRA. Even nonworking spouses are eligible.

1986: The IRA Loses Its Appeal
The Tax Reform Act of 1986 eliminates, in many cases, the tax-deductibility feature that has made

the IRA so attractive to many working Americans. Under the new regulations, many employees who are covered by company retirement plans can no longer deduct their annual IRA contributions.

When this deductibility is eliminated, many investors simply stop contributing to their IRAs. Only the thriftiest of savers (and those who have no company retirement savings plans) continue to contribute.

1997: The IRA Comes Back
Congress passes the Taxpayer Relief Act of 1997, which creates the new Roth and Education IRAs. Both of these IRAs, as well as an "enhanced" original IRA, offer increased benefits to investors. For many, the Individual Retirement Account has become, once again, a smart retirement savings vehicle.

How an IRA Helps to Save for Retirement

IRAs, like 401(k) plans, allow the money that you earn on your annual contributions to grow tax-free within your account until you withdraw that money at retirement. Your earnings will accumulate faster in an IRA, over time, than in a taxable investment earning the same rate of return because your earnings aren't eroded by taxes.

Obviously, an IRA can't be your only retirement savings. The amount that you can contribute annually is limited, so one IRA account won't provide the 60 percent to 80 percent of your pre-retirement income that many experts estimate

F.Y.I.

There are a few additional types of IRAs. If you decide to "roll over" the funds from a qualified retirement savings plan, such as your 401(k), into an IRA, it's called a rollover IRA. A Simplified Employee Pension, or SEP, is a special type of IRA, which you can set up if you're self-employed. (A SEP can also be set up by a small-business owner for employees.) And a Simplified Incentive Match Plan for Employees, or SIMPLE, is another type of IRA, designed for small employers to set up a retirement savings plan for their workers.

Americans will need to retire comfortably. But it is a good place to start if you don't have an employer-sponsored plan, or a next step if you've contributed the maximum to your 401(k) and want to build supplemental retirement savings.

The Traditional IRA

The traditional IRA is sometimes referred to as an ordinary or regular IRA. The two advantages to this type of IRA, which were unchanged by the 1998 tax changes, are:

1. You may be able to deduct some or all of your contributions from your gross income.

2. The money saved in your IRA—including earnings and gains—are not taxed until you take the money out at retirement.

Who Can Open an IRA?

Anyone under age 70½, at any income level, can set up and make annual contributions to a traditional IRA—as long as you earned a salary (or self-employment income) during that year. That means your teenage daughter or your toddler (if she's a child actor perhaps) could open an IRA account. Even if you already contribute to another retirement plan, such as a 401(k) plan, you can still open an IRA. (You may not be able to deduct your contributions, however, if you are covered by an employer retirement plan.)

Who is ineligible, then? A person who has no

salary. If you get all of your income from interest, dividends, and other investments, you cannot open an IRA. The law states that you must have compensation, or "earned" income. The one exception: The nonworking spouse of a married couple may contribute money to a spousal account if the working spouse has an IRA.

Your Contributions

The most you can contribute to an IRA in one year is $2,000. (But if you only earned $1,500 during the year, then you can only contribute $1,500. You can't contribute more than you earn in a given year.) There is no minimum investment amount specified by the IRS, but the mutual fund company or bank that holds your account may set minimum requirements of their own.

Once you open an IRA account, you can make contributions every year (if you qualify). But you don't have to. You can skip a year, or two, or ten, if you choose. You can't make up those payments in future years, however. If you don't qualify to contribute in any given year—let's say that you lived off your investments last year and didn't earn a salary—your account still remains active and continues to grow tax-deferred. You just can't make a contribution for that particular year.

You can make your contributions at any time during the year. In fact, you even have a little extra time to make them. Your contributions for the year must be made by the due date for filing your federal tax return for that year. For most people, in other words, contributions for 1999 must be made by April 15, 2000. (If you receive an income-tax-filing extension, you may be able to put off making your contribution until that extended filing deadline as well.)

Spousal Contributions

If you are married, both you and your spouse can make annual contributions to an IRA. You cannot set up a joint IRA, however. You each must have your own account. Can you both still contribute, though, if one spouse doesn't work for pay (i.e., he or she is a stay-at-home parent)? Yes. You can both still make annual contributions to an IRA even though the stay-at-home parent technically doesn't have any "earned income." This is the one exception to the rule discussed earlier. But, again, your nonworking spouse can't simply contribute to your IRA. He or she must have his or her own IRA.

How much can nonworking spouses contribute? Up to $2,000 per year. That means you and your spouse can make combined IRA contributions of up to $4,000 per year. No more than $2,000 may be contributed to either your IRA or your spouse's IRA in a given year, however. You can't put $3,000 in your account this year, for example, while your husband puts the remaining $1,000 into his account.

Deducting Your Contributions

The deductibility of your contribution to a traditional IRA still depends on two factors: whether you're covered by an employer-sponsored retirement plan, and your adjusted gross income. Thanks to the Taxpayer Relief Act of 1997, however, both of these requirements are now more lib-eral, which means that more people will be able to deduct their IRA contributions.

Are You Covered by an Employer Plan?

This is the first test to see if you can deduct your IRA contributions. If you are *not* covered by an employer-sponsored retirement plan, you can deduct your traditional IRA contribution from your income taxes.

In the past, if you didn't have a retirement plan at work but your spouse did, you were not allowed to take this full deduction. According to the new law, however, you can now take a full deduction if you don't have a retirement plan at work even if your spouse does, as long as you and your spouse's joint adjusted gross income is $150,000 or less.

What does it mean, though, to be "covered" by a retirement plan? This area can be somewhat mis-leading, but it's an important distinction. Believe it or not, you don't actually have to participate in a retirement plan to be considered "covered." According to the IRS, you only need to be "eligible" to participate in your company's retirement plan for you to be considered "covered" by that plan.

Let's say you work for a company that offers a 401(k) plan. You do not contribute to the plan nor does the company make contributions for you. Are you covered, technically? You bet, says the IRS.

That doesn't mean that you can't take the de-duction. It just means that you can't take the *full* deduction.

In other words, you may not be able to deduct all of your contributions if either you or your spouse are covered by a retirement plan at work.

SMART DEFINITION

Filing status

Your filing status depends primarily on your marital status. Are you single, married, divorced, or widowed? If you did not live with your spouse at any time during the year— and you filed a separate return—you are not treated as married. Your filing status is considered to be single, according to the IRS.

What Is Your Adjusted Gross Income?

This is the second test to see if you can deduct your IRA contributions. Even if you are covered by an employer-sponsored plan, you may still be able to take a deduction (either partially or in full), depending upon how much you and your spouse (if you're married) earn, and your filing status. Your deduction begins to phase out as your income rises and is eliminated altogether when it reaches a certain amount. The income amounts vary, depending on your filing status. In other words, you may be entitled to only a partial (that is, reduced) deduction—or no deduction at all—depending upon how much money you earn and what your income tax filing status is.

Here's a simplified version of the income limits:

Adjusted Gross Income	DEDUCTION	
	Single	Married, Filing Jointly
$30,000 and under	Full	Full
$31,000–$40,000	Partial	Full
$41,000–$50,000	None	Full
$51,000–$60,000	None	Partial
$61,000 and up	None	None

Of course, you can still stash money in a traditional IRA even if you're not eligible to deduct the contributions. The benefit: The earnings and gains on that money will continue to grow tax-free until you withdraw it. Another option to consider, however, may be the Roth IRA.

Partial Deductions

You may not be able to take a full deduction for your IRA contribution if you are covered by an employer retirement plan and/or your income falls above certain limits. However, you may qualify for a *partial* deduction. For every $1,000 that you earn above the income limits set by the IRS, your deduction is reduced by about $200 (until you reach the income level at which the deduction is eliminated entirely).

If you are covered by an employer retirement plan, your IRA deduction will be reduced or eliminated depending upon your filing status and your adjusted gross income (AGI), as follows:

If your filing is:	Your IRA deduction is reduced if your modified AGI is between:	Your deduction is eliminated if your modified AGI is:
Single, or head of household	$30,000 and $40,000	$40,000 or more
Married—joint return, or Qualifying Widow(er)	$50,000 and $60,000	$60,000 or more
Married—separate return	$0 and $10,000	$10,000 or more

If you are not covered by an employer retirement plan, but your spouse is, your IRA deduction is reduced or eliminated depending on your filing status and modified adjusted gross income, as follows:

If your filing is:	Your IRA deduction is reduced if your modified AGI is between:	Your deduction is eliminated if your modified AGI is:
Married—joint return	$150,000 and $160,000	$160,000 or more
Married—separate return	$0 and $10,000	$10,000 or more

The Roth IRA

The Taxpayer Relief Act of 1997 created a brand-new type of Individual Retirement Account: the Roth IRA, named after Senator William Roth of Delaware, who championed its passage in Congress.

Like the traditional IRA, this new IRA lets you save up to $2,000 per year in your own account. If you're to qualify as a contributor, however, your income must fall within certain limits. For instance, you *can't* make a contribution to a Roth IRA if your adjusted gross income exceeds:

- $160,000 for married couples, filing jointly

- $110,000 for single filers

With a traditional IRA, by contrast, you can make a contribution no matter what your income level. (You may not be able to deduct the contribution on your tax return, however.)

Your annual contribution to a Roth IRA is not tax-deductible. Ever. (That means your contributions are made with after-tax dollars.) Contributions to a traditional IRA can be tax-deductible, however, depending upon your income level and filing status.

Although you can't deduct your contributions, there are several other important tax advantages to consider with this new IRA:

1. Tax-Free Withdrawals

The Roth IRA, which has been available since January of 1998, is completely tax-free. Investors don't just defer taxes on earnings until withdrawal (as you do with traditional IRAs and most other tax-deferred retirement saving plans). Rather, investors don't have to pay any taxes on withdrawals *at all*, as long as:

• you've invested money in your Roth IRA for at least five years without taking any money out; *and*

• you're over age 59½ when you withdraw the money; *or*

• you're using the money to help pay for a first-time home purchase or other "special" situations if you're under age 59½. (See "Penalty-Free Withdrawals," below.)

This ability to receive tax-free earnings—for your lifetime—could give you more retirement income than you'd have with the traditional IRA. For instance, let's assume that you will invest $2,000 annually. Your investment earns a 9 percent average annual rate of return and you are in a 28 percent federal tax bracket when you put the money in your account and when you take it out. After 20 years, your Roth IRA would be worth $111,529; your traditional, nondeductible IRA, $91,501. After 30 years, your Roth IRA would be worth $297,150; your traditional, nondeductible IRA, $230,748.

To make a fair comparison with the nondeductible, traditional IRA and the Roth IRA, the deductible, traditional IRA value includes the annual tax savings from each year's contribution, which are invested in a taxable investment earning the same return; earnings are taxed every year and the tax liability is deducted from the balance.

SMART MONEY

"A Roth IRA will often yield greater economic benefits than a traditional retirement plan for an individual whose tax rate does not decline after retirement," writes Jeffrey L. Kwall, J.D., in his article "The Value of Tax Deferral: A Different Perspective on Roth IRAs," from the Institute of Certified Financial Planners' *Journal of Financial Planning.*

Making the Most of Your IRA Contribution

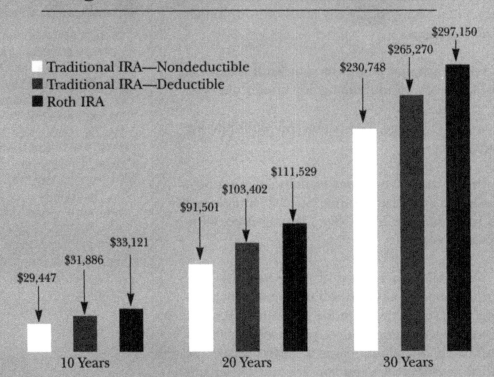

This chart assumes a hypothetical $2,000 annual investment at the beginning of each year, a 9% average annual effective rate of return, and a 28% federal tax bracket for all options at the time of contribution and of distribution.

• **The nondeductible Traditional IRA** includes after-tax contributions which grow tax-deferred until withdrawn at the end of the specified period.

• **The deductible Traditional IRA** includes deductible contributions which grow tax-deferred until withdrawn at the end of the specified period. Plus, to make a fair comparison with the nondeductible Traditional IRA and the Roth IRA, the deductible Traditional IRA value includes the annual tax savings from each year's contribution which are invested in a taxable investment earning the same return; earnings are taxed every year and the tax liability is deducted from the balance.

• **The Roth IRA** includes nondeductible contributions which grow and are distributed tax-free at the end of the specified period.

All values reflect a lump sum distribution at the end of the period net of any applicable taxes and assume no early withdrawal penalties due upon distribution. This hypothetical example is for illustrative purposes and does not represent the performance of any security.

Source: Fidelity Investments. Copyright 1999 FMR Corp. All rights reserved. Reprinted by permission.

2. Penalty-Free Withdrawals

Unlike money withdrawn prematurely from a traditional IRA, you won't pay that 10 percent early-withdrawal penalty if you take money out of your Roth IRA before age 59½. Why? Since your Roth IRA contributions are made with after-tax dollars, you can take that money out without paying a penalty—as long as you've had your account open for at least five years. If you want to withdraw the earnings, too, you may—without incurring a penalty—if you have had your account open for at least five years and you withdraw the money for the following reasons (you can also withdraw money early from a traditional IRA for these reasons):

• **First-Time Home Purchase.** You can withdraw up to $10,000 to help you, your spouse, your children, even your grandchildren foot the bill of a new home. You won't pay any federal income taxes on this withdrawal either if your money has been in your account, untouched, for at least five years.

• **Higher Education.** You can withdraw money to help yourself and those same family members pay for college or other post–secondary education expenses such as tuition, books, supplies, and equipment.

• **Other Special Situations.** You can withdraw money prematurely from a Roth IRA (and a traditional IRA) to pay for some additional expenses. You can withdraw funds prematurely to pay for medical insurance for yourself, your spouse, and your dependents; for example, if you lost your job and have received unemployment for more than 12 weeks. You can also withdraw funds early to pay for unreimbursed medical expenses. However, you can take into account only medical expenses that you would be able to deduct on your income taxes.

3. Flexible Contributions

You can keep making contributions to your Roth IRA as long as you have "earned" income. (See Smart Definition of "Compensation" on page 51.) With a traditional IRA, you can't contribute after age 70½.

4. Flexible Withdrawals

A traditional IRA requires that you take at least a minimum distribution begining at age 70½. (See chapter 9 for a fuller discussion of withdrawals from your traditional IRA.) A Roth IRA, however, has no such requirement. You don't have to start taking your money out at age 70½. In fact, you are not required to take your money out at all during your lifetime. If you want, you can pass your Roth IRA assets on to your beneficiaries. (This doesn't mean that your IRA will pass to your beneficiaries tax-free, however. The earnings will always be free from income taxes, of course. But in most situations your estate will pay estate taxes on your IRA assets.)

The Education IRA

The Taxpayer Relief Act of 1997 created another new type of IRA. Called the Education IRA, this

IRA isn't meant for retirement savings at all. Rather, families can stash up to $500 per year, per child, into this special IRA to help them pay for future college expenses.

Who qualifies? Families with adjusted gross incomes of less than $160,000. For single taxpayers, it's $110,000 or less. Contributions made to an Education IRA are not tax-deductible, but the earnings are tax-free if the money, when it is withdrawn, is used for expenses related to "higher education," which includes tuition, fees, books, supplies, and equipment.

All contributions are made for minors, meaning you can open an account for your child as long as he or she is under 18 years of age. You can't make any more contributions to an Education IRA, however, after your child has reached his or her 18th birthday.

Contributions aren't limited to just parents. Grandparents, aunts and uncles, friends, virtually anyone can make a contribution to a child's Education IRA account.

The only limitation: The total amount contributed for one calendar year cannot exceed $500 per child. It doesn't matter how many Education IRAs are set up for a child. (You can set up as many as you like.) And it doesn't matter how many people contribute to an Education IRA. The annual contribution limit is still $500 for each child. (Those are the current regulations. There is some discussion about raising the annual limit.)

Money in an Education IRA must be used by the time the child reaches age 30. However, money unused in one account may be rolled over into another child's Education IRA. Some glitches: You can't take tax-free withdrawals from this IRA the same year that you use tax credits for college

"The firm that I work for has a SIMPLE IRA. I contribute the maximum allowed every pay period. The money comes out of my check—before taxes—so I never have a chance to miss the money," says Mary Anne Torswick, a 38-year-old legal secretary and mother of two. "What's even better is that the firm contributes 3 percent of my salary, too, at the end of the year. It's like getting a bonus."

spending such as the Hope Scholarship tax credit or the Lifetime Learning tax credit. Also, contributions can't be made in the same year that you make state prepaid tuition plan payments for that same child.

IRAs for Small Businesses and the Self-Employed

A small business may not have the resources to set up a 401(k) plan for its workers. (The plans are expensive to administer.) Instead, the company may set up a simpler retirement account, aptly named the SIMPLE IRA. Another choice for small companies and self-employed workers is the SEP-IRA.

The SIMPLE IRA

The Savings Incentive Match Plan for Employees (SIMPLE) is a retirement plan that was designed for small businesses. Under this arrangement, employees contribute a percentage of their paycheck—similar to the payroll deductions you would make with a 401(k) plan—into an IRA. Under a SIMPLE plan, employees can set aside up to $6,000 each year.

In return for your contribution to a SIMPLE IRA, your employer must make some contribution to your IRA. Your employer has two choices:

1. Match your contributions, dollar for dollar, up to 3 percent of your compensation.

2. Make a "nonelective" or fixed contribution of 2 perent of pay for all eligible employees instead of a matching contribution.

Employees are 100 percent vested in contributions immediately. You decide how your IRA money will be invested, and you keep your IRA account even when you change jobs.

Who's eligible to participate in a SIMPLE IRA? You must be allowed to participate in your company's SIMPLE plan if you:

• Received at least $5,000 in compensation from your employer during any two years prior to the current year;

• Expect to receive at least $5,000 in compensation during the calendar year for which contributions are being made.

Withdrawals from a SIMPLE IRA are subject to the same rules that apply to traditional IRAs. If you withdraw the money before age 59½, for example, you'll incur a 10 percent early-withdrawal penalty. (For more details, see chapter 8.) However, there is a two-year waiting period from the date you first enroll in your company's SIMPLE plan. If you take an early withdrawal before satisfying that two-year requirement, you'll owe 25 percent in penalties rather than the standard 10 percent.

The SEP-IRA

Small businesses and self-employed people can set up a special type of IRA. Called a SEP-IRA, it stands for Simplified Employee Pension IRA. This type of arrangement is actually a pension plan in which contributions are made to traditional IRAs that have been set up for participants in the plan, or separately by a self-employed worker.

Under this plan, you're allowed to put up to 15 percent of your pay (up to $160,000) or $30,000 (whichever is less) into a SEP-IRA each year. In most cases, that's much more than the $2,000 you're allowed to contribute annually to a traditional or Roth IRA.

Small businesses make these contributions on behalf of their workers. A uniform percentage of pay must be contributed for each worker, but businesses are not locked into making contributions each year. How much the company will contribute to a plan each year will depend, probably, on how profitable the company was during a particular year. The decision of how to invest the money (that is, in stocks or bonds), though, is up to you, the employee.

As a self-employed worker, you can also set up your own SEP-IRA. In this situation, you're technically both the employer and the employee. When determining your 15 percent limit on contributions, your compensation is your *net earnings from self-employment*. According to the IRS, that's your gross income earned from your business minus all allowable business deductions. However, you get a little perk with that calculation. Allowable deductions include contributions to your SEP-IRA. In other words, your contributions to your SEP-IRA are deductible expenses for your business.

Who qualifies as a self-employed worker? The requirements are that:

• You are at least 21 years old.

• You received at least $400 in compensation during the year.

• You worked for your employer during at least three of the five years immediately preceding the tax year (if the company is making the contributions and not you, the self-employed person).

Withdrawals from a SEP-IRA are subject to the same rules that apply to traditional IRAs. If you withdraw the money before age 59½, for example, you'll incur a 10 percent early-withdrawal penalty. (For more details, see chapter 8.)

SEP-IRAs can be set up at most of the same institutions that set up traditional IRAs, such as a brokerage firm or a bank. (For more details, see chapter 6.) SEP contributions can be put into stocks, mutual funds, money market funds, and other similar types of investments.

Is an IRA Right for You?

An Individual Retirement Account is one way that you can stockpile savings for retirement. The IRA comes in two basic varieties: the traditional IRA and the Roth IRA. Both offer many tax-saving advantages.

But how do you decide if an IRA is right for

you? And if it is, which type should you pick? Let's compare the advantages and disadvantages of 401(k)s and IRAs, both traditional and Roth.

The IRA versus the 401(k)

Like 401(k)s, IRAs are retirement savings plans. Money contributed to your account grows, tax-deferred, until you take the money out at retirement. Over time, money saved in a tax-deferred account builds up faster than money saved in a taxable account.

Most experts agree, however, that a 401(k) plan is, for most people, a better savings vehicle than an Individual Retirement Account. 401(k)s let you contribute more to your account each year, and they offer an employer match in many cases. IRAs do not. If your employer offers a 401(k), you should probably contribute as much as you can to that account before setting up an IRA.

It's possible that you can contribute to both types of accounts. But the tax savings are less if you do. (See "Deducting Your Contributions" on page 57 for an explanation.) Here is a basic comparison of the two plans:

1. Can You Open an Account?

401(k): Yes, if your company offers a plan, and you meet the plan's eligibility requirements. Each plan will vary, so you must check with your employer.
IRA: Yes, if you had "earned income" (that's salary, wages, self-employment income, even alimony)

during the year, and you are younger than 70½ years old. You can contribute to an IRA if you also contribute to another retirement plan, such as your 401(k).

2. How Much Can You Contribute?

401(k): Each company's plan differs. Your plan will stipulate how much of your income can be deferred each year into your 401(k) account. That amount is determined, in part, by the limits that the IRS sets. In 1998, the IRS limited pre-tax annual contributions to $10,000. (This amount is adjusted annually for inflation.) Although these government regulations limit your 401(k) contributions, you can put more money into a 401(k) account than into an IRA.

IRA: You can contribute up to $2,000 per year to your IRA. If you or your spouse does not earn an income, another $2,000 can be contributed annually to a spousal IRA.

3. Does Your Employer Offer a Match?

401(k): Yes, in many cases.
IRA: No.

4. What about Income Taxes?

401(k): Your contributions to your 401(k) are made with pre-tax dollars. That means the money that you put into these plans is deducted from your paycheck before taxes are withdrawn, so you'll pay less in taxes right now. In addition, you won't pay any tax on the money you're contributing, or the earnings on the contributions made, until you withdraw the money at retirement. At that time, you may be in a lower tax bracket.

IRA: Unlike with your 401(k), the money that you contribute has been taxed. But as with the 401(k), IRA contributions can grow tax-deferred. You don't pay any taxes on your account earnings until you withdraw the money at retirement. Again, at that time you may be in a lower tax bracket.

5. Is Your Contribution Tax-Deductible?

401(k): You can't deduct the amount that you contribute to your 401(k) plan on your income tax return.

IRA: That depends. If your income exceeds certain levels set by the IRS and if you're eligible to participate in a company-sponsored plan such as a 401(k), you cannot deduct your IRA contribution on your tax return.

6. Can You Borrow or Withdraw Funds Before Retirement?

401(k): Yes. Generally, you can borrow funds from your account. And you may also be able to withdraw funds if you qualify for certain "hardship withdrawals," such as medical expenses and college tuition.

IRA: You can't borrow funds from your IRA, but under the new rules, you can withdraw funds—without paying an early-withdrawal penalty—to pay for expenses such as a first-time home purchase and higher education.

The Traditional IRA versus the Roth IRA

Should you choose a traditional IRA or a Roth IRA? That decision will depend on your tax situation and how many years down the road you expect your retirement to be.

The Roth IRA versus the Deductible IRA

First, consider your tax situation. The traditional, deductible IRA gives you an immediate tax deduction, and it offers tax-deferred growth. You will pay taxes in the future, however, when you make withdrawals during retirement.

The Roth IRA, on the other hand, does not offer any immediate tax savings. You don't get a tax deduction with a Roth IRA, but you do get tax-deferred growth. And you don't pay taxes on your contributions or the earnings when you withdraw the money at retirement, as long as you keep the money in your account untouched for five years.

Now, think about when you plan to retire. If retirement is a long way off, the Roth IRA looks more appealing than a traditional, deductible IRA. But if you plan to dip into that IRA within the next few years, a traditional, deductible IRA may be the better alternative.

SMART SOURCES

Need help deciding whether to convert your IRA assets to a new Roth IRA? Check out Fidelity's online IRA Evaluator at:

www.fidelity.com

All you have to do is enter a few variables and the evaluator will project how much money you'd have in the future if you converted your traditional IRA to a Roth IRA now.

Vanguard Investments and T. Rowe Price offer similar assistance—including a Roth IRA conversion calculator—at their web sites:

www.vanguard.com

www.troweprice.com

The Roth versus the Nondeductible IRA

If you're not eligible for a deductible IRA, then a Roth IRA is probably a better alternative for you. (That's assuming, of course, that you fall within the income limits of the Roth IRA.) Why? Initially, you pay the same amount of taxes with a nondeductible IRA as you do with a Roth IRA because neither IRA is deductible. But when you withdraw the funds, the Roth IRA becomes the better deal because you don't pay taxes on the money when it's withdrawn. (The only requirement: You must hold your Roth IRA for at least five years before tapping into it.) You do pay taxes on money withdrawn from a traditional IRA, however, no matter when you take that money out.

The Old versus the New

This is a basic comparison of the traditional IRA and the new Roth IRA:

1. Are You Eligible to Contribute?

Traditional: You must be under age 70½ and earn a salary. The one exception: A stay-at-home spouse can also contribute.

Roth: You can make contributions at any age, as long as you're still earning a salary. (Nonworking spouses can make contributions, too.) Your income must fall within certain limits, however. (See "The Roth IRA" on page 60.)

2. Is Your Contribution Tax Deductible?

Traditional: Yes. But your income must fall within certain limits, and you can't be eligible to participate in your company's retirement plan.
Roth: No.

3. How Much Can You Contribute?

Traditional: $2,000 per person, per year.
Roth: $2,000 per person, per year.

4. What Tax Advantages Do You Get?

Traditional: Deductible contributions are pre-tax dollars. All earnings grow tax-deferred.
Roth: All contributions and earnings grow tax-free.

5. Do you Pay Taxes When You Withdraw Your Funds?

Traditional: Yes. You must pay tax on your earnings and deductible contributions when you withdraw them from your account at retirement.
Roth: You will pay no taxes on the withdrawal of your *contributions,* as long as you have held your account open for the five-year minimum. You will pay no taxes on the withdrawal of your *earnings* if you've held the account open for at least five years and you're older than age 59½ or you're taking the money out for a "special" reason. (See "Penalty-Free Withdrawals" on page 58.)

6. Can You Withdraw Funds Before Retirement?

Traditional: Yes. If you're under age 59½, you'll pay a 10 percent early-withdrawal penalty unless

you withdraw the funds for "special" reasons. (See "Penalty-Free Withdrawals" on page 58.)

Roth: Yes. If you're under age 59½, you'll pay a 10 percent early-withdrawal penalty on the *earnings* withdrawn, unless you withdraw these funds for "special" reasons. (See "Penalty-Free Withdrawals" on page 58.) If you're under age 59½, you can withdraw your *contributions*—penalty-free—as long as you have had your account open for at least five years.

7. When Do You Have to Take Distributions?

Traditional: You must begin taking distributions of your IRA account at age 70½.

Roth: There is no mandatory distribution age. You don't have to take distributions at all during your lifetime; you can pass your account to your heirs.

Converting to a Roth IRA

The Taxpayer Relief Act gave you the options of contributing to an "enhanced" traditional IRA and the brand-new Roth IRA. But it also offers another opportunity: You can convert your existing IRA to a Roth IRA.

If you have a traditional IRA—and if your adjusted gross income is $100,000 or less—you can "convert" your current account to a new Roth account. The downside is that you'll have to pay taxes now on the earnings and deductible contributions that you move from your old IRA into a

Roth account. The benefit, however, is that any future earnings in your Roth IRA will grow tax-free.

In general, a conversion from a deductible IRA to a Roth IRA is probably a good idea if:

• Retirement is many years away. A Roth IRA looks better and better the more years you have to take advantage of that tax-free growth.

• You don't want to make withdrawals from your IRA at age 70½. With a traditional IRA, you must begin taking distributions at age 70½. But with a Roth IRA, there is no requirement for mandatory distributions.

• You have money (outside of your IRA or other retirement savings) to pay for the taxes resulting from a conversion. This way, more money will remain in your new Roth IRA to grow tax-free.

• You expect to be in the same tax bracket, or higher, when you retire. If you expect your tax rate to be higher when you withdraw your money, it may make sense to pay taxes now at your current, lower rate. In the future, when your tax rate is higher, you'll make tax-free withdrawals from your Roth IRA.

Conversely, a conversion from a deductible IRA to a Roth IRA may not be a good idea if:

• Retirement is only a few years away. You need time to recoup the tax money needed to convert your account.

• You don't have the money to pay the conversion taxes. You could take some of the needed funds from your IRA itself. But if you're younger than age 59½ you would have to pay a 10 percent early-withdrawal penalty, and less of your retirement savings will remain in your account, growing tax-free.

Whether you set up a Roth IRA, a traditional IRA, a SEP-IRA, and/or an Education IRA, you put the power of tax deferred savings to work. (With a Roth IRA, of course, you kick those tax savings to the next level: your Roth IRA withdrawals are tax free.) You can use an IRA to supplement your 401(k) savings or as a starting point for your own retirement savings if your employer doesn't offer a 401(k) or if you're self-employed.

THE BOTTOM LINE

If you don't have a 401(k) plan through your employer, or if you want to save supplemental retirement savings, you may want to open an Individual Retirement Account. The newest IRA option, the Roth IRA, offers tax-free growth and requires no mandatory withdrawals at any age. You can convert your traditional IRA to a Roth IRA, if you're eligible. But you don't have to. You can simply leave your existing IRA account as is and open a new Roth IRA for future contributions.

Invest- ment Basics

Congratulations. You've decided to start saving for your retirement by contributing to your 401(k) plan or an Individual Retirement Account. Now comes the difficult part: You have to determine how best to invest those contributions. Should you put your money into stocks, bonds, or both? What about a guaranteed investment contract? How much money should you allocate to each type of investment?

Before you can make such decisions, you need to understand the basic concepts of investing. What are the different types of investment risk, for example? How will dollar cost averaging and compounding affect investments? Why is diversification so important? This chapter will explain these principles and more.

Understanding Investment Risk

If you want to do the things that you've planned in retirement, you'll need a certain amount of money. Unfortunately, to amass that retirement nest egg in today's world, you can no longer rely solely on Social Security benefits, your own savings, or perhaps some assistance from your grown children. You must *invest* your money to reach your financial goals.

The trouble with investing, of course, is that it involves risk. When you make an investment, there's always some chance that you could lose the money that you are investing. How much risk you ultimately take will depend upon several factors:

1. Your Personality. How comfortable do you feel about taking risks? A sudden decline in a stock's price, for instance, could cause some investors to lose sleep at night; other investors might sit back and calmly wait for the market to climb back up. (They might even take advantage of depressed prices and scoop up additional shares.) Your general disposition toward incurring or avoiding risk is called your risk tolerance.

2. Your Age. When you're young, you can generally afford to take more risks because you have more time to recoup your losses if your investments dip in value. As you near retirement age, you may be less inclined to put your retirement money at risk, since you'll soon need to draw on those funds.

3. Your Knowledge. Novice investors are often timid investors. At the first sign of a downturn, they may panic and sell their shares. But as investors become more knowledgeable about the market's fluctuations, they generally learn to handle the ups and downs without panicking.

4. Your Current Financial Status. Are wealthy folks more risk-tolerant than their poorer kin? Not necessarily. Still, if you don't have an extra dime to spare, you may be less willing to take a risk. On the other hand, if you have more room to play around with your budget, you may be willing to take greater risks.

5. Your Time Horizon. How long do you have to reach your financial goals? Generally, the sooner that you need the money, the less risk you can take.

SMART DEFINITION

Conservative or low-risk investor

• I don't want to risk any of my principal.

• I want a guaranteed rate of interest on my investment.

• I am near retirement.

Moderate or medium-risk investor

• I can live with some ups and downs.

• I would like a combination of high- and low-risk investments.

• I have some time for my money to grow.

Aggressive or high-risk investor

• I have an iron stomach and can handle market swings.

• I want the highest possible long-term rate of return, even if I risk losing short-term principal.

• I have at least 10–15 years for my investments to grow.

Source: Life Advice pamphlet, about 401(k) plans. Reproduced with permission of the MetLife Consumer Education Center.

Risks ... and Rewards

Risk is tied to an investment's return. In general, riskier investments reward investors with potentially higher returns. But the flip side is that you have a greater chance of losing money than you do with a conservative investment like a money market account.

Should you simply pick a more conservative investment, then, and avoid having to worry about risk? The trouble with that strategy is that you may play it too safe—and it'll cost you over the long run. The less risk you take, the lower the potential return on your investment. Over time, a too conservative investment could mean that your retirement fund won't grow enough. By the time that you're ready for retirement, you won't have amassed enough money because your investment earned such small amounts that it may not have even kept pace with inflation. If you're young and saving for retirement, you want an investment that will grow your savings—not simply preserve it.

The Volatility Factor

Some investments have steady returns year after year. Other investments are more erratic: One year, the return is up from the average; the next year, it's way down.

Risk is generally measured by the "volatility" of the return on your investment. In other words, investments whose returns swing widely from the average are considered the most volatile.

Those that remain relatively constant are considered conservative. A certificate of deposit, for instance, may offer a return of 5 percent this year. That might be 0.5 percent more than it paid last year. A certificate of deposit is a conservative investment.

A stock, meanwhile, may have an annual return of 20 percent this year. Last year, it might have yielded 13 percent; the year before that, just 9 percent. A stock is, naturally, a more aggressive investment.

Over time, however, even the most volatile investment returns should become more predictable. If you invest in a stock, for instance, the price fluctuations should even out over a 20-year time period.

You can find out exactly how volatile a stock is by doing a little research. Stocks or stock mutual funds are compared to certain indexes (see "Understanding Indexes," below), which are considered the "average." If a stock or stock fund rises (or falls) more than its index, that stock or fund is more volatile than the stock market, on average.

Understanding Indexes

How'd the market do today? Ask that question of any seasoned investor or professional money manager and generally they'll tell you how the Dow Jones Industrial Average (DJIA, or the "Dow") did that day. But what does that mean exactly? Should it concern you and your investments?

An index or "average" tracks the fluctuations in price of a certain type of security, such as the stock issued by a small company or a government bond. That information is useful to you, the investor, because it helps you gauge how well—or how poorly—your own stocks, bonds, or mutual funds are doing by comparison. It also helps you decide when it's wise to buy or sell. If you want to buy blue-chip stocks during a recession, for instance, an index will tell you how such stocks fared in the past under similar economic conditions.

The most widely quoted stock index is the DJIA. You might hear, for instance, that the Dow gained fifty points today or, in the case of Black Monday (October 19, 1987), dropped 508 points. How helpful is that information when evaluating your own portfolio's long-term performance? Not much. The DJIA tells you how the general stock market performed on a given day. Period. Surprisingly, the Dow tracks the movement of just 30 stocks, so it's rather narrowly based. Granted, those stocks are 30 of the largest blue-chip stocks, such as IBM, AT&T, and Coca-Cola; together they represent about 15 percent of the total market value of all the stocks traded on the New York Stock Exchange (NYSE). But they don't show the whole picture.

To accurately assess how your stocks, bonds, and funds are faring, you must compare their performance to an index that reflects the kind of investments you have. If your portfolio consists of nothing but large-company stocks, like the ones that make up the DJIA, then it's a good index for you. But if you hold a variety of small and large, domestic and international stocks, plus some corporate and government bonds, you'll need to look at more than the DJIA to check up on your investments.

Fortunately, market analysts have developed dozens of other stock and bond indexes, ranging from indexes that focus on a particular industry, such as health care or automobiles, to indexes that track five thousand different stocks. You'll find these indexes listed in the *Wall Street Journal* and, often, the business section of your local paper, too.

Many portfolio managers use the Standard & Poor's 500 as a benchmark because it's far broader than the Dow. Comprising five hundred blue-chip stocks (including the DJIA's thirty stocks) that are traded mostly on the NYSE, the S&P 500 is often the index "to beat." That's not so easy to do, however. Often, professional money managers are content if they equal the S&P's performance year after year. Last year, for instance, 17 percent of actively managed general equities funds outperformed the S&P 500.

Small-cap stocks (or stocks of companies whose current stock market value ranges from $250 million to $1 billion) are not included in the S&P 500. To check up on the stock performance of smaller companies, you'll have to look at the Wilshire Small Cap Index or the Russell 2000 Index, which is often considered the best barometer for small-cap stock performance.

Some small-stock investors look to the NAS-DAQ Composite Index, too, which follows some 5,600 stocks traded on the National Association of Security Dealers exchange. Not all those stocks are small, however. But they do tend to be more volatile than the 30 stocks of the Dow.

If you're holding some mid-cap stocks (or stocks whose market capitalization ranges from $1 billion to $5 billion), you'll have to check out the S&P 400 MidCap Index, which tracks, obviously, medium-size stocks. For foreign shares, look to the Morgan Stanley Capital International Europe, Australia, Far East (EAFE) Index. Consisting

Index of Indexes

Basically, there's an index for almost every type of stock or bond out there. Once you know which stocks make up each index, you can choose the index that best matches your portfolio's makeup.

The Dow Jones Industrial Average. The oldest, most frequently cited index, it tracks the movement of just 30 stocks. Of course, those stocks happen to be 30 of the largest blue-chip stocks, such as IBM, AT&T, Coca-Cola, and McDonald's. There's also a Dow Jones Utilities Stock Average and a Dow Jones Transportation Stock Average.

Standard & Poor's 500. Tracks five hundred blue-chip stocks (including the Dow's thirty stocks), which are mostly traded on the New York Stock Exchange. Small stocks are not included. Professional money managers frequently use the S&P 500 as a benchmark that they must beat, or at least equal. There's also an S&P 400 Midcap Index, which tracks four hundred medium-sized stocks.

Wilshire 5000 Index. The broadest index of all, it tracks five thousand stocks. That's all the stocks on the New York Stock Exchange, the American Stock Exchange, and NASDAQ.

Russell 2000. The best benchmark for the stock performance of small companies. Tracks two thousand "small cap" stocks.

NASDAQ Composite Index. Tracks all of the stocks traded on the National Association of Security Dealers Automated Quotations (NASDAQ) exchange.

Morgan Stanley Capital International Europe, Australia, Far East (EAFE) Index. Consists of more than one thousand stocks. The most-watched index of foreign stock performance.

Lehman Brothers Aggregate Bond Index. Represents the average of all public-issued, fixed-rate, nonconvertible government and corporate bonds that are at least Triple B rated. There's also a separate Lehman Brothers Corporate Bond Index and a Lehman Brothers Government Bond Index.

of more than one thousand stocks, it's the most watched measure of foreign stock performance. The only drawback: It's heavily weighted toward Japan and doesn't include any Latin American stocks.

Perhaps the broadest measure of all is the Wilshire 5000 Index. As you might imagine, it tracks five thousand stocks. That's all the major stocks—both large and small—on the New York Stock Exchange, the American Stock Exchange, and NASDAQ. Because it tracks such a variety of stocks, you'd use this index primarily to check up on a balanced fund or an asset allocation fund, both of which invest in a mixture of small and large stocks.

Should you decide to buy and sell the stocks of one particular industry—utility companies, for instance, such as electric, gas, and telephone companies—check out the Dow Jones Utilities Stock Average. If it's railroad and airplane stocks you are angling for, follow the Dow Jones Transportation Stock Average. And if it's bonds you're buying, check out the Lehman Brothers Aggregrate Bond Index. It represents the average of all public-issued, fixed-rate, nonconvertible government and corporate bonds that are at least Triple B rated.

Your Time Horizon

Your risk tolerance will change as you age. In general, the closer you are to retirement—and the sooner you need the money—the less risk you should probably take. Conversely, the farther away you are from retirement, the more risk you can comfortably take.

Why? The more time that you have, the less

that you have to worry about the cyclical nature of the market. You have time for the market to recoup from a downward swing.

When people talk about "time horizon," they often refer to long-, medium-, and short-term investments. They mean that you expect to hold your investments for the following time periods:

- **Long term:** 7 years or more

- **Medium term:** about 5 years

- **Short term:** 3 years or less

Types of Risk

When you're looking at investment risk, keep in mind that different types of investments offer different types of risk. Stock and bond prices fluctuate for many of the following reasons:

Market Risk

This is the risk associated with the ups and downs of the stock market or other financial markets that you're investing in. In the short term, for instance, stocks and bonds are very risky. Their prices fluctuate wildly, and if you're forced to sell when the market is down, you could lose significantly. Over time, however, this risk is lessened if you buy stocks and hold them over the long term. That way, you can be assured of selling your shares when the stock price is up. Historically, stocks have outperformed most other investments over time.

To limit your market risk invest in both stocks and bonds. These assets do not move together: when stock prices are up, bonds are down.

Industry Risk

Industries may perform well (or poorly), depending upon the economy or what's happening in the world. A war, for instance, may help stocks in aerospace companies rise. To hedge against industry risk, you should invest in companies that are in different industries; that is, those that are unlikely to behave in the same way at the same time. Some classic examples of such stock groups include those of banks, computers, airlines, cosmetics, and hospital management. Cyclical stocks, on the other hand, tend to follow the economy. These stocks, which include auto manufacturing companies, steel companies, and paper companies, tend to perform well when the economy is growing, and do poorly when the economy slows down.

Many mutual funds hedge against industry risk automatically because they invest your money in the shares of a number of different companies, in different industries. Not all do, though. Some mutual funds invest exclusively in a particular industry such as technology or health care. If your portfolio includes the latter type of "sector" fund, you should hedge against risk by investing in another mutual fund that invests across different industries.

Business Risk

You've invested in the stock of a particular company. That company is now losing money and, pos-

F.Y.I.

All investments have risk. And there are many types of risk. The key is to find the appropriate type of risk for your "time horizon." For instance, if you're investing for the long term, you should worry about the long-term risk of inflation. Conversely, if you're investing for the short-term, you should worry about the short-term risks of the stock market.

sibly, is in danger of going out of business. That's business risk. This risk can be reduced if you invest in a number of companies rather than a single company. As with industry risk, a mutual fund hedges against business risk because the fund manager invests your money in the shares of many different companies.

Inflation Risk

Inflation erodes the value of a dollar and thus, the value of your investment. Inflation risk is, essentially, that the dollars you invest today won't be worth much when you retire. An investment that can't keep up with inflation will leave you with little purchasing power. It is possible that the return on certain investments will be less than the rate of inflation. Inflation generally runs about 3 percent to 5 percent per year. At certain times, it has soared much higher. During the early 1980s, for instance, the inflation rate was 12 percent.

If you're working with a financial planner, ask if the "projected return" quoted on a particular investment for retirement is the return you'll get *after* inflation is figured into the equation. This will help you see that your investments are keeping pace with (or exceeding) the inflation rate.

Interest Rate Risk

This risk applies to bonds mostly. As interest rates rise, bond prices fall (and vice versa). Bonds are affected the most by changes in interest rates, but interest rates affect the stock market, too. Often, the stock market dips in value when interest rates are high because stocks must compete with higher bond yields.

Credit Risk

Like interest rate risk, this risk mostly involves bonds. The risk is that the issuer of the bond will default on payment to the bondholder. Treasury bonds are the safest; they're backed by the U.S. Government. But junk bonds and high-yield bonds can be risky. As a result, they pay the most interest.

You can protect yourself somewhat from this risk by checking on the financial stability of the bond issuer before making an investment. Moody's and Standard & Poor's provide ratings.

Reducing Your Investment Risk

Risk is part of investing. You can't eliminate it entirely because some of the factors affecting risk, such as the economy and world events, are beyond your control. You can minimize your risk, however, by employing the following tactics:

Diversification

Your mother may not have put her money in anything riskier than a bank account, but her homey motto that you shouldn't put all your eggs in one basket is applicable to the most sophisticated of investments. Different types of investments respond differently to changing market and economic conditions. You'll minimize some of your investment risk if you spread your money among different types of investments.

This investment strategy is called diversification and here's how it works: One type of investment (bonds, let's say) doesn't perform well one year. In that same year, another type of investment (stocks, for instance) has better-than-usual returns. Because the stock portion of your portfolio is doing better than average, you won't feel the hit to your bond holdings as much as you would if your *entire* portfolio was invested in bonds. Losses (or gains) in any particular investment won't make or break you, financially, because the investment is just one piece of your entire portfolio.

Basically, you don't want to dump all of your money into one investment. You want to spread your "risk" around so that if one or two investments sour, they won't drag your entire retirement savings down. It's that simple.

There are two ways to diversify your investments:

1. Invest in Different Types of Assets

Some assets rise and fall in tandem. Other assets move in opposite directions under similar conditions. If you want to diversify, it's often generally recommended that you include securities that act differently under similar cicumstances. A classic example is stocks and bonds. Historically, stocks and bonds have enjoyed an inverse relationship: As bond prices go up, stock prices generally fall.

If you invest in both types of securities, you

won't be betting the ranch on either extreme. The growth potential of stocks will be balanced by the relative stability of bonds. At any given point, some portion of your portfolio will always be performing well.

A typical mix of stocks and bonds for a portfolio is 60 percent in stocks, 40 percent in bonds. But the mixture of stocks and bonds (and cash, if you choose) in your portfolio will depend less on a prescribed formula and more on what level of risk you are comfortable with, how long your investment time horizon is, and what type of investment return you require to meet your financial goals.

With a 401(k), you can generally invest in different types of assets. According to federal rules, your 401(k) plan provider is supposed to offer different types of investments that represent different types of risks. With an IRA, you can generally invest in any type of vehicle that you choose.

2. Buy Several Investments within Each Asset Class

You want to invest in stocks? Fine. Just don't plunk all of your cash into the stock of one company or industry. To lessen your risk, you must diversify within the asset class, too. That means buy stocks or mutual funds that represent different companies and that focus on different industries. Don't buy just Microsoft shares, for instance. And don't limit your diversification to other technology stocks. Consider an automotive, oil, real estate, or pharmaceutical stock, to name a few.

In addition, buy different kinds of stock: large-company and small-company stock, foreign stock and domestic stock. This will help balance your portfolio.

Advantages of Starting to Save Early through a 401(k) Plan

Year	A SUSAN waits 8 years to start saving		B RICHARD starts saving early, quits after 8 years		C BRIAN starts saving early and keeps at it!	
	Annual Investment	Year end value @ 8%	Annual Investment	Year end value @ 8%	Annual Investment	Year end value @ 8%
1	$0	$0	$1,250	$1,295	$1,250	$1,295
2	0	0	1,250	2,694	1,250	2,694
3	0	0	1,250	4,205	1,250	4,205
4	0	0	1,250	5,836	1,250	5,836
5	0	0	1,250	7,598	1,250	7,598
6	0	0	1,250	9,501	1,250	9,501
7	0	0	1,250	11,557	1,250	11,557
8	0	0	1,250	13,777	1,250	13,777
9	1,250	1,295	0	14,879	1,250	16,174
10	1,250	2,694	0	16,069	1,250	18,763
15	1,250	11,557	0	23,611	1,250	35,167
20	1,250	24,579	0	34,692	1,250	59,271
25	1,250	43,713	0	50,973	1,250	94,687
30	1,250	71,827	0	74,897	1,250	146,724

What You Invest and What You Earn

A–started late; 22 yrs. @ $1,250	B–stopped early; 8 yrs. @ $1,250	C–started early & continued; 30 yrs. @ $1,250
Amount Invested $27,500	Amount Invested $10,000	Amount Invested $ 37,500
Investment Income $44,327	Investment Income $64,897	Investment Income $109,224
Total saved $71,827	Total saved $74,897	Total saved $146,724

The figures indicated reflect employee contributions only. In this example, investment return is calculated at 8%. Your own 401(k) investment return may be higher or lower, depending on the performance of the funds offered and how you invested the money in your account.

Source: 401Komics, Product of the 401(k) Association.

Finally, buy stocks that represent different investment styles. You should probably invest in both growth and value stocks. Growth stocks—usually in cutting-edge industries like technology and communications—offer more "growth" (as the name implies) than value stocks, which are generally "undervalued" at the moment. Growth stocks are more volatile than value stocks. If the market tumbles, growth stocks tend to fall harder and faster.

Time

It's never too early to start saving for retirement. The sooner you start, in fact, the longer your money has to grow and the less money you'll actually have to set aside into savings. (See "Advantages of Starting to Save Early through a 401(k) Plan," opposite.) Saving and investing early gives your money a chance to grow—and it's another way to protect yourself against risk.

The stock market (and each business and industry) can fluctuate wildly from one week to the next. But over the course of many years, the stock market has historically provided the best annual returns. To protect yourself against the risk of those short-term fluctuations, though, you need *time* to wait out the downturns.

Compounding

One way that your money grows over time is through a process called compounding. Compounding lets you earn interest on your interest. (You also earn interest on your original investment.) The longer that you let an investment "compound," the more money you'll have.

Here's how it works: Let's assume that you invest $2,000 in a fund this year that earns 10 percent. At the end of the first year, you'll have $2,200 (your original investment plus $200 earned in interest). The following year, however, your money will grow even more. Your original investment will continue to earn that 10 percent annually, but your earnings from that first year (the $200) will earn 10 percent, too. By the end of year two, your total investment value will be $2,420.

$2,000	(your original investment)
$200	(10 percent interest earned on that investment, year 1)
$200	(10 percent interest earned on that investment, year 2)
+ $20	(10 percent interest earned on your interest, year 2)
$2,420	*Total*

The Rule of 72

To better understand how compounding works, you need to understand the "Rule of 72." This simple mathematical formula can help you figure out how long it will take to double your money.

First, you must know how much interest you're earning annually on your investments. Next, divide 72 by that annual rate of interest or earnings. The result? That's how many years it will take for your investment to double.

For example, if you earn 4 percent per year on a certificate of deposit, your initial investment would double in about 18 years. Here's the math:

$$72 \div 4 = 18$$

If you invested that same money in a mutual fund and earned 16 percent per year, you would double your investment in just 4½ years. The math, again:

$$72 \div 16 = 4½$$

Market Timing

Buy low. Sell high. Every investor wants to do that. Trouble is, the stock market moves too quickly, and too often. Even professional money managers can't always time their purchases exactly right.

Market timing is necessary for people who want to make money in the stock market *immediately*. If you plan on investing your money over the long term, however, you don't need to time the market. In the long run, you should still come out ahead because, in the past, the stock market has always come back up again eventually.

Rather than attempting to time the market, individual investors are generally advised to take advantage of another investment strategy. It's called dollar cost averaging. All this means is that you invest the same amount of money, on a set schedule, in a given stock or mutual fund—no matter if the market is rising or falling.

Timing is not an issue. You invest your $50 every other week, for example, regardless of the current stock price. Why is this advantageous? Because you are investing consistently throughout the year, you'll be buying more shares when prices are low, and fewer when prices are higher. Although you are making purchases regardless of price, studies show that investors who use dollar cost averaging tend to pay less per share over time than those who buy shares in a lump sum.

STREET SMARTS

"We do not recommend that participants try to actively manage or *market time* their portfolio. It is almost impossible to successfully market time a portfolio on a consistent basis, and as most studies indicate, this strategy actually detracts from overall returns," says Mark Mullin, vice president and chief investment officer at Diversified Investment Advisors in Purchase, New York.

SMART MONEY

"The rate of return you receive on your investments determines how quickly your money will grow. Risk and return go together. The key is to find the right balance for your goals," says David L. Wray, president of Profit Sharing/401(k) Council of America, in Chicago, Illinois.

If you're contributing to your 401(k) plan, relax. You're already taking advantage of dollar cost averaging. Those regular contributions to your 401(k) plan are automatically deducted from your salary every pay period, without any thought of the purchase price of the stock or fund you're investing in.

Understanding Investment Return

The rate of return, or total return, on your investment reflects how much (or how little) your investment has grown. Your investment's total return consists of interest or dividends paid, plus the change in the value of the stock, bond, or mutual fund itself. In general, total return is an annual figure and is given as a percentage. The average annual total return on one small-cap stock fund, for example, was 10.53 percent last year.

When selecting investments, you must consider their rate of return. But how can you know upfront how your investments will perform in the future? Let's rephrase that. When selecting investments, you must consider their *expected* rate of return. While you obviously can't predict the future, you can look at past returns of investments and make an educated guess as to what you expect them to do in the future.

Every financial planner on the planet will tell you that past performance is no guarantee of future returns—and they're right—but historical data can give you some perspective. For instance, growth stock funds have provided, over the past five years, an average annualized rate of return of 18.63 percent. It would be reasonable for you to assume, then, that if you invested in those types of stocks in your retirement fund you could expect a similar return over the long term. (If you're investing for a short time period, it's harder to estimate because stock prices can fluctuate dramatically.)

Now, how does this total return number figure into the retirement equation, and why is it so important? When you sit down to plan your retirement investments, you must calculate how much money you'll need for retirement. (Most experts say that you'll need from 60 percent to 80 percent of your current income in your retirement years.)

Let's say, for example, that you need $900,000. To achieve that nest egg, you'll have to save. There are three factors that will affect the amount you save:

1. The amount that you contribute annually

2. The number of years that you make those contributions

3. The rate of return that you receive on your investments

When combined correctly, these three variables will generate the size of the nest egg that you need. Let's assume, however, that you're contributing as much as you can—without jeopardizing your other financial obligations—but it's not enough to reach your goals. How to make up for this shortfall? Put your money into investments that will earn a higher rate of return. Consider a higher-risk investment that will return 10 percent rather than the lower-risk

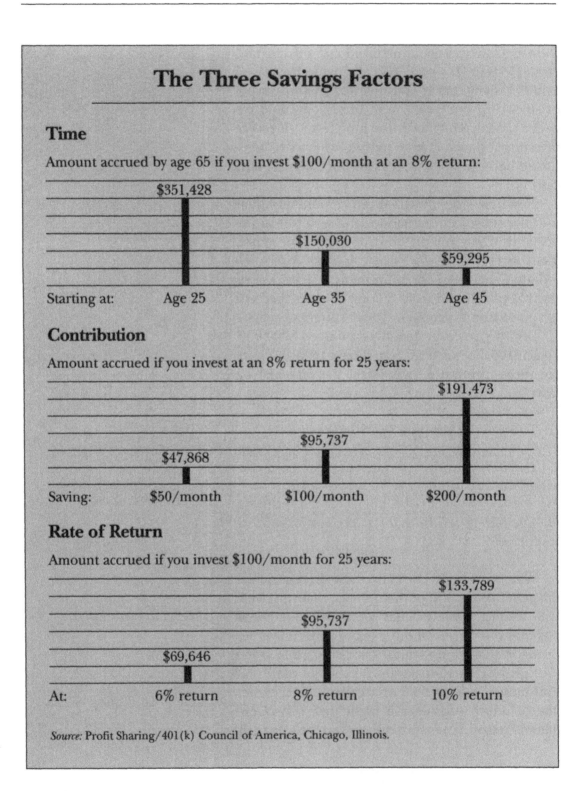

The Three Savings Factors

Time

Amount accrued by age 65 if you invest $100/month at an 8% return:

$351,428

$150,030

$59,295

Starting at: Age 25   Age 35   Age 45

Contribution

Amount accrued if you invest at an 8% return for 25 years:

$191,473

$95,737

$47,868

Saving: $50/month $100/month $200/month

Rate of Return

Amount accrued if you invest $100/month for 25 years:

$133,789

$95,737

$69,646

At: 6% return   8% return   10% return

Source: Profit Sharing/401(k) Council of America, Chicago, Illinois.

investment that is currently earning 7 percent. Even an additional one percentage point of return can substantially boost your savings.

How Much You Need to Save

How much money do you need to save to generate the kind of income that you want in retirement? That depends on a host of variables: your age; your current salary; how much you've already saved; how much you expect to receive from Social Security; and so on.

A financial planner can help you figure this out. (It's rather complicated, though. Inflation, taxes, and your expected investment return must be added into the calculation.) Or you can run the numbers yourself, using one of the numerous retirement planning software programs currently available.

Your employer may be able to offer some assistance, too. As part of your 401(k) package, many plan providers offer a retirement calculator and other tools designed to help you estimate your future retirement income needs and set savings targets.

If you have Internet access, you can find some retirement savings calculators online. The Mutual Fund Education Alliance, a trade organization, offers retirement worksheets at its web site (www.mfea.com), as do some mutual fund companies. Fidelity Investments (www.fidelity.com), for instance, provides a calculator and other helpful information; Vanguard (www.vanguard.com) offers

SMART MONEY

To estimate how much your lifestyle during retirement will cost you, consider the following widely held assumptions and how they could affect you:

• Your home mortgage may be paid off and you may move into a smaller home at retirement.

• Expenses for your children will have decreased, including the major responsibility of paying for a college education.

• The cost of health care will probably rise and so may your need for medical care.

• Leisure and travel costs may increase.

Source: Mutual Fund Education Alliance, Kansas City, Missouri. Reprinted with permission.

Navigator Plus, a free retirement software package, through its Retirement Resource Center.

The beauty of any of these "calculators" is that you can play around with the numbers a bit—what would happen if you saved more, for example, or if you invested in more aggressive investments. The result: You'll get an idea of whether you're saving enough, or how far off the mark you are. For many, it may be just the wakeup call that you need to start saving.

The table on page 103 should give you a rough idea of how much money you'll need in your retirement.

To meet your retirement needs, you will have to develop an investing strategy that works for you. Keep in mind that every investment carries some risk, however. By spreading your money among a variety of investments, you will minimize your portfolio's overall exposure to risk. You will also increase your chances of earning a return that will produce a total savings that will allow you to retire comfortably.

What Will It Take to Maintain Your Standard of Living in Retirement?

Current Age	Current Income	Additional Funds Needed
	$120,000	$2,280,161
40	$80,000	$1,407,087
	$40,000	$552,839
	$120,000	$1,312,274
50	$80,000	$776,278
	$40,000	$251,842
	$120,000	$737,095
60	$80,000	$408,049
	$40,000	$85,024

Note: Assumes 15 years of retirement; 4 percent inflation; 4 percent annual growth in current income; retirement income equal to 70 percent of pre-retirement earnings; maximum Social Security benefits; pension equal to 35 percent of retirement income; 8 percent pre-tax return and 28 percent federal tax bracket.

Source: Mutual Fund Education Alliance Investor's Center, on the web at www.mfea.com. Reprinted with permission.

THE BOTTOM LINE

Money is the biggest retirement concern that most people have. Thanks to the proliferation of 401(k) plans and other retirement savings vehicles like IRAs, however, you can build a hefty retirement nest egg by taking advantage of these tax-deferred savings vehicles.

The sooner you start saving for retirement, the better. Because of the effects of compounding, the younger you are when you start investing for retirement, the less money you'll actually have to save.

CHAPTER 5

....

Invest-
ment
Choices

So . . . you think you want to invest in stocks? Are you interested in a small-cap stock or a blue-chip stock? Domestic or international stocks? A stock that pays dividends or a stock that doesn't?

The investment opportunities available today can make your head spin. It is difficult for investors to pick and choose from so many options. Before you decide where to invest your 401(k) or IRA money, you should first understand the types of investments available and how they can help you meet your retirement goals. What follows, then, is a mini-course in stocks, bonds, and other types of investments.

Cash and Cash Equivalents

The term *cash* means more than the money in your pocket. Cash refers to investments that are liquid. In other words, you can get your hands on this money fast, unlike with stock, for instance, where you have to wait to sell. In addition, cash refers to investments that are safe. These are, in fact, the safest investments in town. The risk of your investment rising or falling in value is minimal.

Trouble is, cash equivalents (or cash investments), which include money market accounts, bank Certificates of Deposit (CDs), bank savings accounts, Treasury bills, and Series EE bonds, offer a very low rate of return. In most cases, cash investments earn little more annually—before taxes—than the rate of inflation.

Why select this type of investment? For one

thing, a cash equivalent is a good parking spot for money that you are waiting to invest elsewhere or money that you'll need in the very near future. In addition, cash investments are generally protected, up to a certain amount, by the Federal Deposit Insurance Corporation (FDIC), so there is no risk of losing your principal (your initial investment).

Some cash investments include the following:

• **Bank Savings Account.** Offered by most banks and credit unions. The interest rate is generally very low. (Also known as passbook accounts.)

• **Certificate of Deposit (CD).** Unlike with a bank savings account, money in a CD must stay in your account for a set period of time. At the end of that time, you're guaranteed a stated interest rate, which is typically higher than the rate offered on a savings account. If you withdraw the cash early, you'll pay a penalty in most cases. Generally, the interest rate will increase the more money that you invest in a CD and the longer you keep the money there.

• **Money Market Deposit Account.** These bank accounts require a minimum deposit. You'll pay a penalty if your account balance falls below a specified level. A money market deposit account generally earns a higher rate of interest than a passbook savings account but a lower rate of interest than a CD.

Don't confuse this type of account with a *money market mutual fund.* (See page 116.) A money market deposit account is offered by a bank and is FDIC insured. A money market mutual fund, by contrast, is offered by a mutual fund company. It is not FDIC insured.

SMART MONEY

"The key to successful management of your assets is self-discipline and a reasonable investment of time and effort. But suppose that through smarter investing, you raised your average annual return by only 4 percent. In 18 years, the individual earning 12 percent will have twice the assets of an individual earning 8 percent," advises John D. Markese, Ph.D., president of the American Association of Individual Investors.

• **U.S. Treasury Bill (T-Bill).** T-bills are sold in increments of $10,000 and have maturities of three, six, or twelve months.

T-bills are purchased at a discount and redeemed at their maturity value (that's the value of the T-bill when it comes due). How much do you earn with a Treasury Bill? Your earnings equal the difference between the discounted price that you paid for the T-bill and the amount that you collect at maturity.

• **Series EE Bond.** Commonly called savings bonds, Series EE bonds are available in dollar amounts ranging from $50 to $10,000. You purchase a savings bond for half its face value (a $100 bond costs $50, for instance). In recent years, savings bonds have enjoyed a resurgence because your earnings may be tax-free if you bought the bond after 1989 and you use the money to pay for certain education expenses.

• **Guaranteed Investment Contract (GIC).** A GIC, or a stable value fund, works much like a certificate of deposit (CD). It is offered by an insurance company through your 401(k) plan. Under this arrangement, you are guaranteed a fixed interest rate over a certain time period. The value of your principal (that's the amount invested in a GIC) remains constant—it doesn't fluctuate, as stock and bond prices do—and is repaid, like a CD, at the end of the investment term.

Unlike a certificate of deposit, which is guaranteed by the Federal Deposit Insurance Corp (FDIC), however, a GIC is only guaranteed by the insurance company that issues it. For that reason, your "guarantee" is only as good as the insurance company that's issuing it. If the insurance company fails, you could lose some money. In general, that means you'd probably receive a lower interest rate than originally promised.

The real danger with a GIC, though, is that, like other cash investments, you won't earn enough to beat inflation over time. Although GICs often pay a slightly higher interest rate than other cash investments, you're likely to earn a better return with stocks and bonds—over the long term—than with a cash investment such as a GIC.

Stocks

Stocks, or equities, represent ownership in a company. When you invest in a stock, you buy a share of ownership in the corporation that is issuing the stock. That corporation could be a large, well-known company like IBM, or it could be a tiny start-up, which has been in business for only a few years.

As a shareholder, your investment will rise—or fall—depending upon how well the company does at any given time. If the company has a banner year, for instance, the share price is likely to go up. If the company has a lackluster year, the share price may drop.

Over time, stocks have the potential to produce higher returns than most other investments. But stocks also carry greater risk than most other investments because stock prices fluctuate from day to day. That's why you can't invest heavily in stocks if you need the money *tomorrow*. If the market dips—and you have to cash your shares in—you'll probably lose money. But if you can hold your shares until the market comes back up

SMART DEFINITION

Bear market

A sharp decline in the value of most stocks

Bull market

The opposite of a bear market; stock prices go up.

SMART DEFINITION

Securities

The term *securities* includes a broad range of investment instruments, including stocks and bonds, mutual funds, and options.

Stock Measurements

The Price Earnings Ratio: This calculation, which is commonly referred to as the P/E ratio, tells whether a stock is overvalued. Here's how to figure it: Divide the stock's market price by its current earnings. The higher this ratio, the greater the chance that the stock is overpriced.

Market Capitalization: This measurement tells you how large a company is, based on the price of its stock. It is commonly referred to as capitalization or simply, cap. Here's how capitalization is frequently calculated: Multiply the current market price of the company's stock times the total number of outstanding shares.

Investment professionals use this calculation to classify stocks of various companies. If you invest in a small-cap, mid-cap, or large-cap fund, for instance, that means that all of the fund's money is invested in companies that are a certain size. The definitions of the different caps may vary slightly from one source to another. There is no "definitive" definition.

Until recently, Morningstar, the independent investment information and anaylsis firm, had always classified the three "caps," using pre-specified market cap cutoffs. For instance, a small-cap stock had a market capitalization of less than $1 billion; a mid-cap stock had a market capitalization of $1 to $5 billion; a large-cap stock had a market capitalization of more than $5 billion. Now Morningstar ties its definition of market cap more closely to the relative movements of the market, as follows:

Large-Cap Stocks: The top 5 percent of the five thousand largest domestic stocks in Morningstar's equity database.

Mid-Cap Stocks: The next 15 percent of the five thousand largest domestic stocks in Morningstar's equity database.

Small-Cap Stocks: The remaining 80 percent of the five thousand largest domestic stocks in Morningstar's equity database (as well as companies that fall outside the largest five thousand).

again—and, historically, the market has always revived—you'll come out ahead.

You'll make money with stocks by:

- **Receiving Dividends.** Many companies share some of their profits with shareholders. This is called a dividend.

- **Earning Capital Gains.** The hope is that, over time, your stock will appreciate in value, so that when you sell your shares, you'll make a profit. (Basically, you want to buy low and sell high.) This profit earned when you sell your stock is called a capital gain.

Publicly traded common stocks are bought and sold on stock exchanges such as the New York Stock Exchange in New York (NYSE), which is also commonly referred to as "the Big Board." It's the largest securities exchange in the United States. The American Stock Exchange (AMEX), which is the second largest exchange, is also in New York.

Some stocks are not sold on an exchange at all. Rather, they're bought and sold "over the counter" through a computerized network called NASDAQ (the National Association of Securities Dealers Automated Quotations).

Investors who buy or sell securities on an exchange or over the counter usually do so with the help of a brokerage firm. The investor will deal directly with a stockbroker, who is a representative of the firm.

Some types of common stocks you'll find traded on the stock exchanges include the following:

- **Growth Stocks.** These stocks are issued by companies that are growing at a faster-than-average

SMART MONEY

Here's some good advice from the Vanguard Group of Valley Forge, Pennsylvania, on choosing large- or small-cap investments: "If you seek capital growth and can tolerate wide price fluctuations, you could place more investments on the small-cap side of the [investment] spectrum. If you are more conservative and want some income to accompany growth, your holdings could tilt to the right, toward large-cap stocks. Because large companies account for most of the total cash value of U.S. stocks, many experts recommend that investors avoid concentrating their stock holdings too heavily in the mid- or small-cap arena."

Source: Copyright 1998 The Vanguard Group. Reprinted by permission from *Vanguard Index Trust.* All rights reserved.

pace. Every year, they make more money. (Or that's the expectation, anyway.) Over a long period of time, successful growth stocks outpace inflation by a wide margin. But these stocks are risky in the short term because they're volatile. Over a short period of time, growth stocks can rise and fall dramatically.

• **Blue-Chip Stocks.** These stocks represent older, more established companies that frequently pay high dividends but are not growing as fast as growth stocks. They're generally considered to be "stable" stocks because they provide steady earnings growth. The stocks listed in the Dow Jones Industrial Average are blue-chip stocks.

• **Income Stocks.** Like blue-chip stocks, income stocks aren't growing as fast as growth stocks. That means that they're also less volatile. You won't earn as large a capital gain with this type of stock as you would with a growth stock, but income stocks do pay dividends.

Bonds

A bond is a loan. When a company or the government issues a bond, they are basically writing an IOU to raise money. You lend money to the issuer—by making an investment in a bond—and, in return, receive a fixed rate of interest for a stated period of time. When the bond matures—in 10 or 20 years, or whenever the maturity date is—you receive your initial investment back (referred to as your principal).

Bonds are often referred to as fixed-income investments because a bond pays you a "fixed" income. For example: You buy a $1,000 bond that pays 5 percent interest. Every year that you hold the bond, you receive $50. That amount remains constant for the life of the bond because your income is fixed.

Bonds are often used to diversify an investment portfolio. Their fixed income can help balance the fluctuations of the stock portion of your portfolio. In addition, bonds are often a good way to save for short-term goals. You can match the bond's maturity to the date when you'll get the money.

Over the long term, however, bonds are generally not as good an investment as stocks because they don't provide as much growth. The longer the maturity of a bond, in fact, the greater the risk that your investment won't outpace inflation.

What's more, if you sell your bond before maturity, you may lose money. Why? Bonds have an in-

Bond Basics: Terminology

Face Value: Also called the par value, this is the amount that appears on the face of the bond. It is the amount of your original investment, or principal. You should receive this amount in full if you hold a bond until maturity (unless the bond has a call feature, which means that the issuer can pay off the bond before maturity).

Maturity Date: The bond issuer promises to repay your principal on this date. You don't have to hold a bond until maturity. If you cash in early, however, you may not the get the full value of the bond.

Coupon: This is the interest rate that the bond issuer pays you annually or semiannually, for the life of the bond.

Bond Basics: The Ratings System

Bonds are assigned letter grades by rating agencies to indicate their creditworthiness. Two frequently cited rating agencies are Moody's Investor Service and Standard & Poor's Corporation:

S&P	Moody's	Meaning
AAA	Aaa	Extremely strong/ Best quality
AA	Aa	Very strong/High quality
A	A	Strong/Upper-medium quality
BBB	Baa	Adequate/Medium quality
BB	Ba	Speculative/Below investment grade
B	B	Below investment grade
CCC	Caa	Poor standing
CC	Ca	Highly speculative
C	C	Lowest grade

verse relationship with interest rates: When interest rates rise, bond prices fall.

For example: You need the cash, so you decide to sell your bond before maturity. But interest rates have risen to 8 percent since you bought your bond, and the interest paid on your bond is 6 percent. Who wants your bond? No one. To cash it in, you'll have to sell your bond at a discount. The bottom line: You, the investor, lose money.

Bonds are graded according to their issuer's ability (or willingness) to repay your money at maturity. They are given letter grades, which indicate their creditworthiness, by rating agencies such as Moody's Investor Service and Standard & Poor's (S&P). A high-quality bond is awarded an AA by S&P; an Aa by Moody's. (See "Bond Basics: The Rating System," opposite.) Bonds with lower investment ratings will generally pay higher interest rates than bonds with higher ratings. Junk bonds, for instance, pay very high interest rates because they're issued by companies whose financial stability is shaky.

Bonds are available in several different types. Some possibilities include:

• **U.S. Government Securities** are issued by the federal government. These bonds are backed by the U.S. Government, so they're considered to be a very safe investment. Not surprisingly, that safety translates into a lower interest rate than is paid on other bonds.

Treasury bonds (T-bonds) mature in 10 to 30 years and are purchased as long-term investments. The minimum investment: $1,000. Treasury notes (T-notes) mature in 2 to 10 years. The minimum investment: $1,000 for the longer-term notes; $5,000 for shorter-term notes.

• **Corporate Bonds** are issued by corporations. Generally, a corporate bond pays a higher rate of return than a government bond because there's a higher risk that the corporation will default on payment of the bond at maturity. Corporate bonds can have a call feature, which lets the company "call," or redeem, its bond before maturity. You may not receive the full value of the bond if it's called before maturity.

A junk bond is a corporate bond. However, the

F.Y.I.

Stocks, bonds, and cash aren't the only kinds of investments. Some people invest in pork bellies, which is an investment called a commodity. Other people invest in real estate. And still others invest in collectibles, such as Art Deco jewelry or Depression-era glassware. These investments can be profitable, but since you can't invest your 401(k) or IRA money in these types of investments, we've limited our discussion of investments to the three major investment categories described here in this chapter.

companies that issue these bonds tend to have low quality ratings. As a result, they pay higher interest rates.

• **Municipal Bonds** are issued by states, cities, and other municipalities. These are usually bought for long-term investments. Municipal bonds are attractive to investors because the annual or semiannual interest payments received are generally free from federal income tax. Many municipal bonds have a call feature similar to that of corporate bonds.

• **Zero-Coupon Bonds** don't pay any interest until they mature. However, you must pay tax on the interest earned each year, as though you had actually received it. These bonds are sold for substantially less than their face value. You might buy a $10,000 bond for $5,000 now and redeem it ten years hence for its full face value. Zero-coupon bonds are often used for long-term investments.

Mutual Funds

If you don't want the anxiety of buying and selling individual stocks or bonds, you can buy into a mutual fund. Under this arrangement, individuals pool their money into a large fund managed by investment professionals. Rather than buying shares in just one company, you buy shares in a variety of companies. Instantly, you own a portfolio of different stocks or bonds.

Mutual funds are very popular because they offer professional money management. (That can be very helpful if you're just starting out as a investor.)

Generally, you don't need a lot of money to invest. Most mutual funds require a minimum investment of $1,500 to $2,000, but many waive that requirement if you agree to have money automatically transferred from your checking account to the fund every month.

Mutual funds are a simple way to help you diversify your investments. There are three basic types of mutual funds: stock mutual funds, bond mutual funds, and money market mutual funds. As you might imagine, each of those funds invests in a variety of either stocks, bonds, or money market instruments.

Within each category, however, there are numerous choices, and in some cases there is even some crossover between categories. Generally, mutual funds are classified according to their investment objectives. If you're shopping for a bond fund, for instance, you could consider one of the following:

• **Corporate Bond Fund.** Invests in bonds from corporations.

• **International Bond Fund.** Invests in bonds from foreign corporations.

• **U.S. Government Bond Fund.** Invests in long-term U.S. Government bonds.

• **Municipal Bond Fund.** Invests in bonds issued by cities. Usually, these are long-term bonds, which are free from federal tax.

• **Junk Bond Fund.** Invests in low-grade corporate bonds.

SMART SOURCES

The Securities and Exchange Commission (SEC) offers numerous personal finance publications to individual investors, including *What Every Investor Should Know* and *Invest Wisely: An Introduction to Mutual Funds.*
    Contact the SEC at:

450 5th Street, N.W.
Washington, D.C.
20549-0213
800-732-0330
www.sec.gov.

If you're in the market for a stock fund, some possible choices include:

• **Aggressive Growth Fund.** Tends to invest in small and medium-sized companies that are expected to grow dramatically. A generally volatile fund that has the potential of a very high rate of return.

• **Growth Fund.** Invests in companies that are growing at a faster-than-average rate. Not as volatile as an aggressive growth fund.

Study the Prospectus

The prospectus is a document that explains what you need to know about your mutual fund. By law, the mutual fund company must send you a copy of the prospectus before you invest. And you must sign a statement, before you can buy shares in a fund, that says you've read the prospectus thoroughly.

Most prospectuses are written in language that is somewhat reader-friendly. You'll still find plenty of confusing InvestmentSpeak, but you can always call the mutual fund company and ask for an explanation. The content and format of each prospectus are similar since the Securities and Exchange Commission imposes minimum reporting requirements. In a prospectus, you'll learn:

• **The Fund's Objectives.** The prospectus should state clearly *how* the fund invests its money and what its overall investment strategy is. For instance, a prospectus for one stock mutual fund states clearly:

Goal: Long-term growth of capital.

Strategy: Invests mainly in common stocks of well-known and established companies.

Who May Want to Invest: The fund is designed for those who are looking for an investment that focuses on well-known, established companies.

- **Growth and Income Fund.** More conservative investment than a pure growth fund, this invests in companies that provide dividends and steady growth.

- **Index Fund.** Invests in stocks that reflect a certain index, such as the S&P 500. By imitating the investment mix of a particular index, an index fund hopes to provide the same return (or higher) as the index it represents.

- **Sector Fund.** Invests in a specific industry such as computers or biotechnology.

- **The Fees Involved.** All prospectuses are required to include a fee table, which lists the fund's expenses. These fees can include an annual maintenance fee, a sales charge for the purchase of the shares (which is called a load), and redemption fees (levied, in some cases, when you sell). If you buy a no-load mutual fund (that means there is no fee up front for the purchase of shares), you might be charged a 12b-1 fee instead. This is an annual sales load, too, but many investors don't realize that they pay it because it's not charged up front and it doesn't specifically say "sales charge." 12b-1 fees must be listed in the prospectus.

- **The Financial Highlights.** This can be the most confusing section—unless you're a seasoned investor or an accountant. You'll find figures that state the "net asset value." This simply shows the value of your fund shares at year end. "Portfolio turnover rate" tells you how fast the fund manager buys and sells the stocks or bonds that make up the fund.

- **The Performance History.** Mutual fund performance is commonly measured as total return, or the change in value of an investment over a certain time period. The prospectus will provide annual total return figures for the past 10 years. These figures will be compared with appropriate benchmarks, such as the S&P 500, and, in some cases, the Consumer Price Index, which is a measure of inflation calculated by the U.S. Government.

- **Your Account.** The prospectus will also tell you how to set up your account, what the minimum investment requirement is, and how to buy and sell shares.

SMART SOURCES

Investment Information Online

CNNfn
www.cnnfn.com
The television network's web site offers personal finance features and current business and market news updates.

SmartMoney
www.smartmoney.com
The Wall Street Journal's magazine of personal finance offers information about stocks, bonds, and mutual funds.

Mutual Fund Education Alliance
www.mfea.com
Provides information about no-load and low-load mutual funds as well as special investment features such as Investing for Children, Retirement Investing, and Women and Investing.

• **Balanced Fund.** Invests in both stocks and bonds. By investing in both stocks and bonds, the fund provides both growth and stability.

• **International or Foreign Stock Fund.** Invests in companies located outside the United States. Often this type of fund is used to balance the performance of domestic stocks.

• **Small Company (or Small Cap) Fund.** Invests primarily in the stock of small companies.

If you're interested in a money market mutual fund, you could consider:

• **Goverment Money Market Fund.** Invests in Treasury bills.

• **Tax-Exempt Money Market Fund.** Invests in short-term municipal securities.

Money market mutual funds generally earn a higher rate of interest than a bank savings account or even a bank money market account. Another advantage: check-writing privileges, which generally let you write up to three checks per month (in most cases the check must be for a minimum of $500 or so).

Picking a Mutual Fund

Don't know which mutual fund to select? There's a plethora of information available to the public by different means to help you pick the fund that's right for you:

Call, Write, or Visit the Web Site of the Mutual Fund Companies

They'll send you sales literature and a prospectus, which explains the fund's investment goals, its performance history, and other information. Some of the larger fund companies include:

Fidelity Investments
82 Devonshire Street
Boston, MA 02109
800-544-4774
www.fidelity.com

The Vanguard Group
P.O. Box 2600
Valley Forge, PA 19482
800-662-7447
www.vanguard.com

T. Rowe Price Associates
100 East Pratt Street
Baltimore, MD 21202
800-638-5660
www.troweprice.com

Scudder Kemper Investments
345 Park Avenue
New York, NY 10154
800-225-2470
www.scudder.com

American Century Investments
P.O. Box 419200
Kansas City, MO 64141-6200
800-345-2021
www.americancentury.com

F.Y.I.

When evaluating the performance of a mutual fund, look at the three-year, five-year, and ten-year total returns. Then compare these total returns with the total returns of similar funds.

One-year total return may not give you as accurate a financial picture. One year may not be long enough to accurately assess a fund's performance. The fund manager may have just had a good or bad year.

Check Out Financial Magazines

Publications such as *Business Week, Forbes, Worth,* and *Kiplinger's Personal Finance* periodically report on long-term mutual fund performance, according to a variety of measures.

Consult Low-Cost Mutual Fund Guides

The following guides offer contact information, analyses of funds, and other useful information:

• *Individual Investor's Guide to Low-Load Mutual Funds* ($24.95; free with membership). Provides an analysis of more than eight hundred funds:
American Association of Individual Investors
625 North Michigan Avenue, Suite 1900
Chicago, IL 60611-3110
800-428-2244

• *Directory of Mutual Funds* ($10). Provides address, phone number, and the name of the investment adviser on the mutual funds that are members of the Investment Company Institute:
Investment Company Institute
1401 H Street, NW, 12th floor
Washington, D.C. 20005
202-326-5800

Contact Investment Firms

The following firms are excellent sources. But the material they produce is generally costly, so you may want to borrow these materials from the library instead of purchasing them:

• *Morningstar Mutual Funds.* This twice-monthly newsletter surveys the performance of nearly 1,300 mutual funds. Morningstar rates each fund, using a "risk-adjusted" star rating system ($495 for a year's subscription; you can also buy their review of one particular fund for $5):

Morningstar, Inc.
225 Wacker Drive
Chicago, IL 60606
800-735-0700
www.morningstar.com

• *The Value Line Mutual Fund Survey.* Provides information on more than 1,500 funds. Each fund report is updated three times per year, but you'll receive biweekly ratings on all funds. (A three-month trial subscription is $49; a six-month subscription is $155.) Gives a stock's history, including price fluctuations over time:

The Value Line Mutual Fund Survey
220 East 42nd Street
New York, NY 10017
800-284-7607
www.valueline.com

Still struggling with all of this Wall Street talk? Investing isn't rocket science, but it does take time and effort to understand the terms and nuances. If this is your first brush with investing, consider this an opportunity to educate yourself. Learn as much as you can about investing from your employer, from books and magazines, and by doing research at the library or on the Internet. Study the potential rewards and risks associated with each different type of investment. Don't be afraid to ask questions. And don't be afraid to take some time to absorb the information that you've gathered. Smart investment decisions aren't made overnight.

THE BOTTOM LINE

You have a variety of investment options to choose from today. Some promise greater returns; some offer less risk. The investment vehicles that you pick, be they stocks, bonds, or cash, will largely determine the ultimate value of your retirement savings.

CHAPTER 6

Investing Your 401(k) or 403(b) Plan

• Asset allocation, or how your savings are allocated among various investments, is the single biggest factor in determining your investment success.

• You should diversify your 401(k) savings among different asset classes and within each asset class. This will minimize your overall risk and maximize your return.

• Within your 401(k) plan, you'll be offered a number of different investment options. Your choices will vary from conservative to aggressive. Most employers offer a variety of mutual funds. Some companies also offer the option of buying company stock.

• Where should you invest your 401(k) contributions? It's up to you to pick the investments that are appropriate for you.

Once you decide that you want to participate in your company's plan, you must then make another decision: How should your 401(k) contributions be invested? With a 401(k) plan, you are in charge of your own investments.

Does that thought intimidate you? For many people, saving through a 401(k) or 403(b) plan is their first attempt at investing. It certainly can seem daunting to suddenly be responsible for picking a stock fund and other investments that, if chosen wisely, will build a sizable retirement nest egg.

Most 401(k) plans, though, don't offer every single type of investment currently available, so your investment choices are more limited than if you were simply investing on your own. Increasingly, employers have plenty of information on hand that explains the investment options available through your plan. It's up to you, then, to read, ask questions, and learn as much as possible about investing so that you can make the most of your 401(k) investment.

Asset Allocation

Once you understand the different kinds of investments that are available, you can begin to build a portfolio. In the last chapter, we discussed the importance of diversifying your portfolio among different kinds of investments. Diversification is key to successful investing because it spreads out your investment risk and, thus, cushions the blow if any one asset class should decline in value.

What percentage of your money should go into each of these various investments? The correct mixture, which depends on several variables, such as your age, your financial goals, and a comfortable level of risk, is called asset allocation. By allocating your money properly into cash, bonds, and stocks, you will minimize the risk of loss and maximize your returns.

Your portfolio's asset allocation should not stay the same forever. You may find that an investment mix works well for a number of years. (Or you may find that what worked last year won't meet your needs this year.) In general, though, an investment mix that was appropriate when you were 25 won't be appropriate when you're three years away from retirement.

The biggest factors in determining your asset allocation are risk and time horizon:

• **Risk.** How much risk can you bear—without panicking? Take the "Risk Tolerance Quiz" on pages 128–29 to find out.

• **Time Horizon.** How long do you plan to keep your money invested? That's your time horizon. If you have a long period of time to invest your money—and you can tolerate the ups and downs of the market—most experts would advise that you allocate a good percentage of your portfolio to stocks. If you have a shorter time horizon, you may want to consider cash or bonds.

One common asset allocation for investors with a long time horizon is 40 percent in bonds, and 60 percent in stocks. But that might not work for you. Perhaps you would like a higher return and can tolerate more risk? Then you might want to consider investing in a greater percentage of stocks. In that case, your asset allocation may be 80

SMART DEFINITION

Asset allocation

A term that financial planners and money managers frequently use. It simply refers to the mixture of investments in your portfolio and how much money is invested in each different type of investment, or asset class, to minimize your overall risk. The specific allocation of your particular portfolio will depend upon your age, your financial goals, the risk involved, market conditions, and your desired rate of return.

A Risk Tolerance Quiz

The following quiz, devised by Scudder Kemper Investments, helps investors assess their "risk tolerance." Circle the letter that corresponds to your answer.

1. Just 60 days after you put money into an investment, its price falls 20 percent. Assuming none of the fundamentals have changed, what would you do?
    1a. Sell to avoid further worry and try something else.
    1b. Do nothing and wait for the investment to come back.
    1c. Buy more. It was a good investment before; now it's a cheap investment, too.

2. Now look at the previous question another way. Your investment fell 20 percent, but it's part of a portfolio being used to meet investment goals with three different time horizons.
    2a. What would you do if the goal was 5 years away?
        a. Sell.
        b. Do nothing.
        c. Buy more.

    2b. What would you do if the goal was 15 years away?
        a. Sell.
        b. Do nothing.
        c. Buy more.

    2c. What would you do if the goal was 30 years away?
        a. Sell.
        b. Do nothing.
        c. Buy more.

3. The price of your retirement investment jumps 25 percent a month after you buy it. Again, the fundamentals haven't changed. After you finish gloating, what would you do?
    3a. Sell it and lock in your gains.
    3b. Stay put and hope for more gain.
    3c. Buy more; it could go higher.

4. You're investing for retirement, which is in 15 years. Which would you rather do?

4a. Invest in a money market fund or guaranteed investment contract, giving up the possibility of major gains, but virtually assuring the safety of your principal.

4b. Invest in a fifty-fifty mix of bond funds and stock funds, in hopes of getting some growth, but also giving yourself some protection in the form of steady income.

4c. Invest in aggressive growth mutual funds whose value will probably fluctuate significantly during the year, but have the potential for impressive gains over five or ten years.

5. You just won a big prize! But which one to choose? It's up to you.

5a. $2,000 in cash.

5b. A 50 percent chance to win $5,000.

5c. A 20 percent chance to win $15,000.

6. A good investment opportunity just came along, but you have to borrow money to get in. Would you take out a loan?

6a. Definitely not.

6b. Perhaps.

6c. Yes.

7. Your company is selling stock to its employees. In three years, management plans to take the company public. Until then, you won't be able to sell your shares and you will get no dividends. But your investment could multiply as much as 10 times when the company goes public. How much money would you invest?

7a. None.

7b. Two months' salary.

7c. Four months' salary.

Key: Each *a* answer is worth one point; each *b* answer is worth two points; each *c* answer is worth three points. Total them to get your final score and determine your profile:

9 to 14 points: You're a conservative investor.

15 to 21 points: You're a moderate investor.

22 to 27 points: You're an aggressive investor.

Source: Scudder Kemper Investments. Reprinted with permission.

SMART DEFINITION

Asset class

Common stocks, bonds, and cash (or short-term securities) are the three major "asset classes," or categories of investments. These broad asset classes can be subdivided into smaller classifications. For instance: Bonds could be Treasury bonds, municipal bonds, or corporate bonds. Stocks could mean blue chips, small caps, or mid caps.

percent in stocks, and just 20 percent in bonds. (Even if you're a very aggressive investor, some money should be invested in bonds or cash to cushion you against the market's fluctuations.)

Your asset allocation should reflect your individual needs and goals. Everyone has different investment needs, so, unfortunately, there isn't a perfect asset allocation formula. But you can use "model" portfolios, which are based on various factors such as your age and your risk tolerance, as a guide. Your 401(k) plan provider may include some sample portfolios in the literature you receive when you sign up to contribute. Below, you'll find some helpful model portfolios, which were designed by Scudder Kemper Investments for investors saving for retirement. These models include three types of investors—Conservative, Moderate, and Aggressive—and are arranged according to three age groups—investors "Getting Started," "Prime-Time Earners," and those "Soon to Retire."

Getting Started

This age group includes investors between the ages of 25 and 40; they have a long time horizon.

Conservative

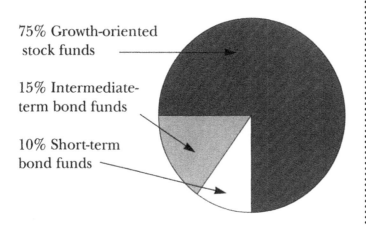

75% Growth-oriented
stock funds

15% Intermediate-
term bond funds

10% Short-term
bond funds

You should consider investing 75 percent of your money in growth-oriented stock funds. You might consider a growth and income fund and/or a growth fund. (A growth and income fund invests in bonds and income-paying stocks.) Since you're a conservative investor, you'll probably want to allocate the remaining 25 percent of your portfolio to bonds: 15 percent in an intermediate-term corporate bond fund and 10 percent in a short-term bond fund. These bond funds will help reduce fluctuations in the value of your investments and will add diversification.

Moderate

80% International &
domestic growth-
oriented stock funds

20% Intermediate-
term & short-term
bond funds

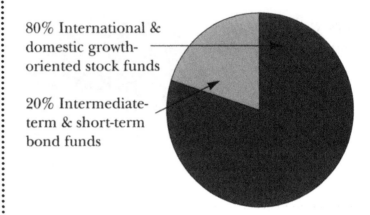

Consider investing 80 percent of your money in international and growth-oriented stock funds; the remaining 20 percent to bond funds, such as an intermediate-term and a short-term bond fund. This offers income, stability, and diversification.

Aggressive

30% International stock
funds

30% Large-company
stock funds

25% Small-company
stock funds

15% Intermediate-term
bond funds

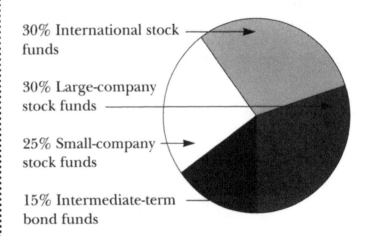

Depending on your age and risk tolerance, it might be right to invest 85 percent in stock funds. You should invest in a diversified mix of stocks in small, large, and international companies. One possibility: 30 percent in an international stock fund; 25 percent in a small-company fund; and 30 percent in a large-company fund. The remaining 15 percent should be allocated to an intermediate-term corporate bond fund, which will provide some income and stability to your portfolio.

Prime-Time Earners

These are investors aged 40 to 55, who still have a long time horizon and are in prime earning years.

Conservative

60% Small-company funds, Int'l. growth funds, growth & income funds

20% Intermediate-term bond funds

10% Short-term bond funds

10% Government-backed mortgage funds

Sixty percent of your money could be invested in a small-company stock fund, an international growth fund, and a growth and income fund. For the remainder of your portfolio, consider a combination of an intermediate-term bond fund (20 percent), a short-term bond fund (10 percent), and a government-backed mortgage fund (10 percent).

Moderate

65% International & domestic growth funds, funds with income-paying stocks & bonds

35% Intermediate-term & short-term bond funds, government-backed mortgage funds

Sixty-five percent of your stock allocation could be invested in international and domestic growth funds as well as a growth and income fund. The remaining 35 percent of your portfolio could be allocated to a combination of intermediate-term and short-term corporate bond funds as well as a government-backed mortgage fund.

Aggressive

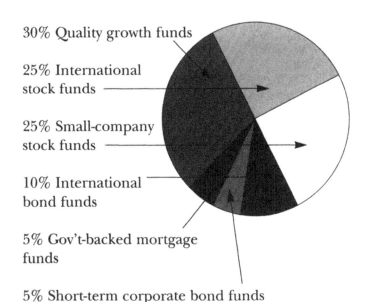

30% Quality growth funds

25% International
stock funds

25% Small-company
stock funds

10% International
bond funds

5% Gov't-backed mortgage
funds

5% Short-term corporate bond funds

You may still want to allocate a large portion of
your portfolio to stocks, in which case you should
invest in a diversified mix of stocks in small, large,
and international companies, such as: 25 percent
in an international fund; 25 percent in a small-
company fund; and 30 percent in a growth fund.
Allocate the remaining money to bonds: 10 percent in an international bond fund; 5 percent in a
short-term corporate bond fund; and 5 percent in
a government-backed mortgage fund.

Soon to Retire

This age group includes investors aged 55 to 65. Although they are nearing retirement, their investment strategy should still focus on growth of their assets.

Conservative

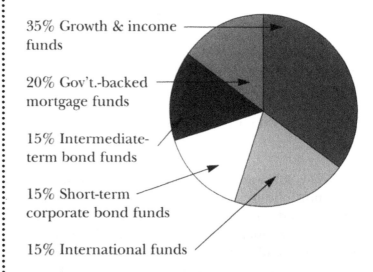

35% Growth & income funds

20% Gov't.-backed mortgage funds

15% Intermediate-term bond funds

15% Short-term corporate bond funds

15% International funds

Half of your portfolio will still be invested in stocks; the other half, in a combination of bonds and cash. To maintain a diversified mix of stocks, invest 15 percent in an international stock fund and 35 percent in a growth and income fund. The other half of your portfolio could be invested in a combination of intermediate-term bond funds (15 percent), short-term bond funds (15 percent), and a government-backed mortgage fund (20 percent).

Moderate

40% Growth & income funds

15% International funds

15% Intermediate-term bond funds

15% Short-term corporate bond funds

15% Gov't.-backed mortgage funds

Fifty-five percent of your portfolio will still be invested in stocks; the remainder should be invested in bonds and cash. To maintain a diversified mix of stocks, invest 15 percent in an international stock fund and 40 percent in a growth and income fund. The remainder of your portfolio should be invested in intermediate-term (15 percent) and short-term (15 percent) corporate bond funds and a government-backed mortgage fund (15).

SMART MONEY

Here's some advice on rebalancing from David Wray, President of the Profit Sharing/401(k) Council of America in Chicago, Illinois:
   "Rebalancing your portfolio keeps your investments on track. It smooths out volatility and gives you a more predictable rate of return. In addition, it forces you to sell high and buy low. But 80 percent of participants last year didn't make any asset allocation decisions at all. Ideally, you should rebalance twice a year. Pick two days, six months apart, and rebalance your portfolio at those times. That way you won't make your decision based on current market conditions."

Aggressive

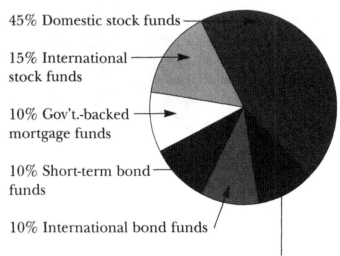

45% Domestic stock funds

15% International stock funds

10% Gov't.-backed mortgage funds

10% Short-term bond funds

10% International bond funds

10% Intermediate-term corporate bond funds

More than two-thirds of your portfolio could still be allocated to stocks. For example: 15 percent in an international fund and 45 percent to domestic stock funds. The remainder of your portfolio should be allocated to an international bond fund (10 percent), a short-term bond fund (10 percent), a government-backed mortgage fund (10 percent), and an intermediate-term corporate bond fund (10 percent).

Keep Your Eye on Your Asset Allocation

Stock, bond, and money market funds perform differently over time and offer different returns.

Some investments will do better than others and, thus, may push your desired asset allocation out of line.

For instance: Let's assume that you've chosen an asset allocation of 60 percent in stocks and 40 percent in bonds. A year has passed since you set up those investments. During that time, the stock portion of your portfolio has done very well, but the bond portion has not. As a result, stocks now make up 70 percent of your portfolio and bonds make up 30 percent (rather than the desired 60 percent–40 percent mix).

You could leave this new investment mix as is. Perhaps you feel that your portfolio should be more heavily weighted toward stocks. Now may be a good time to revise your investment strategy.

This new asset allocation may carry too much risk for you, however. If that's the case, you will have to "rebalance" your investments to reach your original mix. You can accomplish this in two ways:

1. Move some of your investments around. Shift enough money from the stock funds into the bond funds so that you once again have 60 percent of your portfolio allocated to stocks and 40 percent allocated to bonds.

2. Keep your existing investments in place. Instead, alter the allocation of new money invested in your fund. To retain that 60 percent–40 percent asset allocation in your overall portfolio, you will have to allocate a smaller percentage of your new investment money to stocks and a greater percentage to bonds.

To keep track of your portfolio's asset allocation, use a simple worksheet, such as the sample on page 140. Review it periodically.

Sample Worksheet: Your Asset Allocation

Type of Investment	Amount	Percent of 401(k) Savings
Cash		
Money Market Fund		
Guaranteed Investment Contract (GIC)		
Total Cash:		
Bond Funds		
Short-Term Bond		
Intermediate-Term Bond		
Long-Term Bond		
Bond Index		
Other		
Total Bond Funds:		
Stock Funds		
Growth		
Growth and Income		
Aggressive		
International or Global Equity		
Balanced		
Index		
Company Stock		
Other		
Total Stock Funds:		

You can determine the percentage of your savings in each investment category rather easily. Divide the category total (stocks, for instance) by the total amount of money in your 401(k). For example: Let's say that you have a total of $10,000 invested in your 401(k). If $5,000 of that total amount is invested in stocks, then 50 percent ($5,000 ÷ $10,000 = 50 percent) of your plan's assets are allocated to stocks.

Your 401(k) Investment Options

Within your 401(k) plan, you'll be offered a number of different investment options. Your choices will vary from conservative investments to more aggressive ones. Most employers offer a variety of mutual funds. According to Hewitt Associates' 1997 survey of 401(k) trends, plan sponsors offer, on average, eight investment options to participants. (See "One Company's 401(k) Investment Menu," on page 142 for an idea of what may be offered.) Many publicly held companies also offer the option of buying company stock.

It's up to you to pick the investments that work best for you. As you look over the options available, think about which asset class, or investment category, is appropriate for you. Then carefully consider the particular offerings within that asset class. For instance, if you would you like to invest in stocks, check out the types of stock investments that are available. If it's funds, which are right for you?

The types of funds you're likely to find in a typical 401(k) plan include:

SMART MONEY

"Not only do you want to diversify your money among different asset classes, but you also want to be sure to diversify within each asset class. The better diversified you are in each asset class and within each investment option, the better protected you are from any one investment option going bad—thus dragging your entire nest egg down with it," advises Diversified Investment Advisors of Purchase, New York.

F.Y.I.

Employers are not required to offer a specific number of investment options in a 401(k) plan. But most companies offer at least three different funds.

One Company's 401(k) Investment Menu

A good 401(k) plan will offer participants a number of investment choices, ranging from a conservative money market option to an aggressive stock mutual fund. The investment options offered by the following company will meet a variety of investment needs and levels of risk tolerance for the plan's participants:

Short-Term Securities
Stable Value
Money Market Fund

Bond Funds
High-Quality Bond Fund
Government Corporate Bond Fund
High-Yield Bond Fund

Stock Funds
Equity Growth Fund
Growth and Income Fund
Equity Income Fund
Special Equity Fund
International Equity Fund
Aggressive Equity Fund
Stock Index Fund

Strategic Allocation Funds
Short-Horizon Strategic Allocation
    Fund
Short/Intermediate-Horizon Strate-
    gic Allocation Fund
Intermediate-Horizon Strategic Al-
    location Fund
Intermediate/Long-Horizon Strate-
    gic Allocation Fund
Long-Horizon Strategic Allocation
    Fund

Source: Diversified Investment Advisors, Purchase, New York.

• **Money Market Fund.** The assets of a money market fund generally consist of U.S. Treasury Bills, Certificates of Deposit, and other "safe" securities. It is one of the lowest-risk funds that a 401(k) plan offers. This is an extremely safe investment that's appropriate for a conservative investor who's nearing retirement or who wants to add some stability to his portfolio.

• **Guaranteed Investment Contract (GIC).** This fund, which is offered by an insurance company, guarantees a fixed interest rate over a certain time period. The value of a GIC doesn't fluctuate, as stock and bond prices do. The interest paid is generally higher than the interest paid on a money market fund. GIC, which are sometimes called "stable value" funds, can add some stability to a portfolio and may be an appropriate investment for a particularly conservative investor who's just getting started.

A GIC is not guaranteed by the federal government, as its name implies. It is merely guaranteed by the insurance company that issues it. For that reason, your "guarantee" is only as good as the insurance company that's issuing it. A GIC's credit rating should be included in the materials you receive when you enroll in your 401(k). If not, you'll want to do your own research. Insurance companies are rated by companies such as Moody's, A. M. Best, and Standard & Poor's, and you can usually find the publications at your local library.

• **Bond Fund.** Bond funds tend to be less volatile than stock funds, but they are extremely sensitive to interest rate fluctuations. Many investors who invest primarily in stocks like to diversify some of their savings into a bond fund to lower their portfolio's overall risk. The majority of 401(k) plans offer some type of bond fund: a short-, intermediate-, or long-term bond fund or an index bond fund.

• **Aggressive Growth Fund.** These funds invest in the stocks of companies that are expected to grow faster than average. Growth funds and aggressive growth funds offer the promise of high returns

SMART SOURCES

Want advice about where to invest your 401(k) dollars? Check out two Internet-based services, 401k Forum and Financial Engines. Both offer retirement plan advice to the members of the Southwest Airlines' Pilots Association and employees of Fujitsu America, Blue Shield of California, and Alza Corp. Employees log on and the services offer a personalized asset allocation plan, based on the funds offered by the participant's 401(k). Each site has a visitor's section that is accessible to the general public.

401k Forum
www.401kforum.com

Financial Engines
www.financial
  engines.com

SMART SOURCES

Need some comic relief? The 401(k) Association in Bellefonte, Pennsylvania, has introduced a comic book series that addresses a variety of 401(k) issues, such as loans and hardship withdrawals and what to do when you leave your employer.

In the first issue of 401 Komics, Indiana Jones–style adventurers meet Tax Rex, who threatens to "bite" their savings. A 401(k) plan is their only protection. Later the adventurers must choose one of the "footpaths of fluctuation." The first, money markets, is easiest but longest. The last, stocks, is the fastest but has the most risk.

over the long term. These stocks seesaw over the short term, however, so they're probably not a good pick for investors nearing retirement who need their money in the next year or two.

• **Growth Fund.** These funds invest in relatively stable and established companies. While these funds aren't considered as high risk as aggressive growth funds, the share price will fluctuate over the short term. Long term, you have the potential to earn a high return. Often a good choice for long-term investors.

• **International Fund.** These funds invest in the stocks of foreign companies. One advantage to adding such a fund to your portfolio: diversification. Domestic stocks and foreign stocks don't move in tandem. When domestic stocks have a bad year, foreign stocks generally do better.

Don't confuse a global fund with an international fund. Global funds invest in stocks of any country, including the United States. An emerging markets fund is a particular kind of international fund. It invests in Third World or developing countries.

• **Balanced Fund.** Most balanced funds are invested in a combination of stocks, bonds, and some cash. This type of fund can be attractive to inexperienced investors because it's fairly conservative. You have some exposure to the stock market, but the fund probably won't be as volatile as a pure stock fund because it also invests in bonds and holds some reserves in cash.

• **Stock Index Fund.** Index funds mirror the investment mix of a particular investment market, such as small-company stocks or technology stocks. If you buy an index fund that mirrors the stocks included in the Standard & Poor's 500, for instance, that fund should perform as well, or as poorly, as the index itself performed that year. These funds are often a good choice because they're easy to understand and they generally post better-than-average returns. Vanguard 500 Index Fund, which has been open since 1976 and is the oldest index fund available to individual investors, is rated four stars by Morningstar.

• **Growth and Income Fund.** These funds invest in the stocks of established U.S. companies that have good "growth" potential and that frequently pay dividends ("income"). They are generally a good investment for relatively conservative folk who want long-term growth.

• **Asset Allocation Fund (or Lifestyle Fund).** These funds invest in a variety of assets, such as stocks, bonds, and money market instruments. Unlike a balanced fund, which keeps a "fixed" percentage of assets invested in stocks and bonds, an asset allocation fund can change its mix, depending upon market conditions.

Most investors can do their own asset allocation by buying stocks, bonds, and cash equivalents in individual funds. But if you don't want to select your own mix of investments, or if you feel you don't know how to do it, this fund can do it for you.

• **Company Stock.** Some companies offer their own stock as an investment option in their 401(k) plan. In the 401(k) plans that offer company stock as an investment option, almost half of the companies, according to Hewitt Associates' 1997 survey,

SMART MONEY

"In plans that offer employer stock as an investment option, the number one mistake that people make is putting 100 percent of their account balance in employer stock," says David Godofsky, principal, Bryan Pendleton Swats & McAllister, an employee benefits consulting firm in Nashville. The CEO talks up the company and its potential, so participants often can't help but ask themselves, "If it's such a great stock, shouldn't I put 100 percent of my money into it?" "Very rarely is that the correct option," says Godofsky. "Twenty-five percent or less belongs in employee stock. You need some diversification."

WHAT MATTERS, WHAT DOESN'T

What Matters

• The single biggest factor in determining your investment success is asset allocation.

• You're responsible for investing your 401(k) contributions. Your choices will depend on your age, your risk tolerance, your investment time horizon, and your financial goals.

What Doesn't

• Your plan only offers a few investment options. That's okay, as long your 401(k) offers a good stock option and a good fixed income option such as a bond fund or a GIC.

• Trying to buy and sell at the right time—known as market timing.

• Luck and other factors.

require that matching contributions be invested exclusively in the company stock.

While you may feel more comfortable investing in your company stock than another investment (you do know a lot about the company, after all), doing so will mean that the growth of your investment depends entirely on how well the company does.

If your company stock is highly rated (check out the Value Line Investment Survey, which rates stocks), buy some of it. But don't buy any more of it than you would of any other single company. If you put a lot of money into your company stock (or any other single stock), your portfolio won't be very diversified.

401(k) Asset Distribution Trends

According to the Spectrum Group of San Francisco, there has been a marked shift in 401(k) assets from guaranteed and stable value investments to equities, driven by strong stock market performance and investment education programs for participants. The table opposite and the graph on page 148, drawn from a study of one thousand plan participants nationwide, illustrates the movement of these types of funds into more aggressive investments.

Allocation of 401(k) Plan Contributions Among Investment Choices

	1998	1996	1994
Equity Choices			
Long-term growth	14.6%	16.3%	15.9%
Growth & income	15.9%	14.5%	14.6%
Aggressive growth	15.8%	15.8%	11.4%
International/Global	5.3%	6.1%	4.0%
Index	8.2%	5.9%	5.8%
Company stock	10.8%	11.5%	9.8%
Balanced/Total Return:	4.6%	3.2%	6.2%
Bond Choices			
High-yield bond	1.7%	1.2%	1.1%
Intermediate/long term	1.4%	1.4%	2.0%
Corporate bond	0.4%	0.8%	0.9%
U.S. Government bond	1.6%	1.9%	2.1%
Short-term bond	0.4%	0.8%	0.6%
Stable Value Choices			
Guaranteed	5.7%	9.6%	12.7%
Money market	3.6%	4.9%	5.1%
Asset Allocation/Life Cycle			
Higher risk	4.3%	2.4%	2.9%
Moderate risk	3.0%	1.7%	3.1%
Lower risk	1.8%	1.2%	1.8%
Single Asset Allocation Choice	0.1%	0.3%	NA
Self-Directed Brokerage Account	0.6%	0.6%	NA

Source: Spectrem Group, San Francisco, California; copyright 1998.

THE BOTTOM LINE

It's unavoidable. As a 401(k) participant, you are responsible for investing your own contributions. How you invest your money, though, may be more important ultimately than the particular funds that you invest in. Asset allocation, or how your savings are allocated among the various investment options offered through your plan, is the single biggest factor in determining your investment success. According to a Nobel Prize–winning study, the specific investments you choose within each asset class may account for a mere 3 percent of your port-folio's long-term investment return.

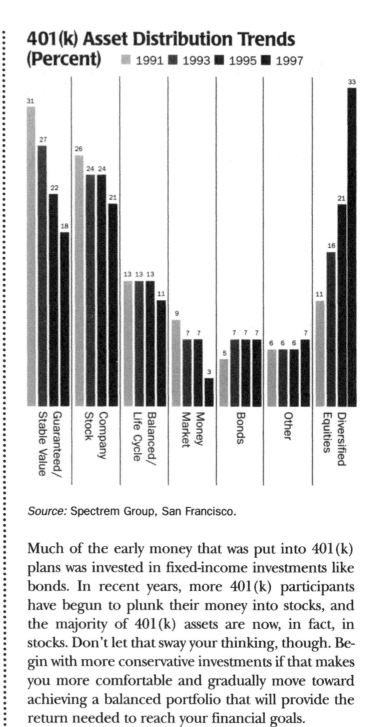

401(k) Asset Distribution Trends (Percent)
■ 1991 ■ 1993 ■ 1995 ■ 1997

Source: Spectrem Group, San Francisco.

Much of the early money that was put into 401(k) plans was invested in fixed-income investments like bonds. In recent years, more 401(k) participants have begun to plunk their money into stocks, and the majority of 401(k) assets are now, in fact, in stocks. Don't let that sway your thinking, though. Begin with more conservative investments if that makes you more comfortable and gradually move toward achieving a balanced portfolio that will provide the return needed to reach your financial goals.

Investing Your IRA

When you contribute to a 401(k), you must decide where you will invest your savings. Should you put your money into a "safe" money market account that will yield a return that barely beats inflation, or should you take on a bit more risk and invest in a stock mutual fund that promises a heftier return on your money?

Similarly, when you open an Individual Retirement Account, you must decide where you will invest your savings. With an IRA, however, you're not limited to the eight or so investment choices typically offered by your employer through a 401(k). You can establish an IRA at almost any kind of financial institution, such as a bank, a brokerage firm, or a mutual fund company. And you can generally pick from a very broad range of investments that these institutions offer.

Your IRA Account

You can open a new IRA each year. You can have 52 different IRA accounts—or more—in fact, if you like. The only requirement: You cannot contribute more than the annual limit of $2,000 to all of your accounts combined in any one year.

Why would anyone want so many IRAs? Okay, you probably don't want 52 accounts, but you will want a few different ones. Here's why:

• **Diversification.** That important investment rule doesn't apply to just 401(k)s. You need to minimize your risk by "diversifying" your money among different asset classes and by buying several investments within each asset class.

Let's imagine that you set up your first IRA this year. You decided to put $2,000 into an aggressive stock mutual fund. Next year, that $2,000 (plus earnings) will remain in that same stock fund. But to minimize some of the risk due to the fluctuations in the market, this year you may set up another IRA and invest this new money in a bond fund. By the third year, you may want to put more money into stocks. But you want to diversify within stocks (the asset class), so you set up yet another IRA. This time it's a growth stock fund. You now have three IRAs and a portfolio that's invested in aggressive stocks, growth stocks, and bonds.

• **You have a rollover.** When you change jobs, you take your 401(k) money with you. But to avoid paying taxes and penalties if you're not age 59½ yet, you must "roll over" the money into an IRA. (For a more complete explanation of a 401(k) rollover, see "Transferring Your 401(k) Assets to Your IRA," page 159.)

You don't want to simply dump the assets into an existing IRA, however. For tax purposes, it's generally best to keep your rollover money in a separate account. That way, if you want to put the rollover money into another employer's 401(k) at some point in the future (assuming that it's allowed by the new employer), you'll be permitted to do so because you didn't commingle the assets.

One drawback to having a lot of IRAs is that it gets expensive. You're generally charged an annual maintenance fee of up to $50 for each IRA, so you could spend a few hundred dollars in annual maintenance fees if you have 10 or so IRAs. Some firms will waive the maintenance fee, but generally only if you have $10,000 or more invested.

SMART DEFINITION

Individual Retirement Account

A retirement savings plan through which you can save money in a variety of investments. Despite the use of the word *account* in its name, an IRA is *not* an investment itself. That means you must open an IRA at a mutual fund company, for example, which will then invest the money in, say, a stock index fund.

Who's the Trustee, or Custodian?

Legally, an IRA is a trust, or custodial, account. That means a trustee, or custodian, such as a bank, a federally insured credit union, a savings and loan association, or some other institution approved by the IRS, will accept your IRA contributions and maintain your account. The custodian will file the necessary paperwork on your account with the Department of Labor and, for tax purposes, the Internal Revenue Service.

The custodian makes sure that your contributions are invested in whatever way you've decided (for example, in a money market fund, if that's the investment you've picked). The custodian also makes sure that you get disbursements from your IRA, upon request. However, the custodian is not responsible for making sure that you contribute to your account each year or that you contribute the allowable amount. That's your responsibility. The bank or credit union merely takes your money and keeps track of it.

Your IRA Investment Options

The money in your IRA can be invested in a great number of investments, including most stocks, bonds, and money market securities. There are some limitations, though. You can't use the money in your IRA to buy a life insurance policy or real estate. Nor can you use the money to buy collectibles, art, jewelry, gold, silver, diamonds, or other precious gems. Options trading is generally restricted and you can't buy commodities futures either. Assets in your account cannot be combined with other property. Still, you have plenty of investment options available. You can set up an IRA at a number of different institutions, including the following:

Your Company IRA

Your employer, labor union, or other employee association can set up a trust to provide IRAs for its employees or members. That means you may be able to open up an IRA at work. Some companies let you take automatic payroll deductions from your paycheck to fund your IRA. For many folks, that convenience makes this an attractive way to save.

The trouble with an on-the-job IRA is that your investment choices may be limited. It will depend upon which mutual fund company or bank is sponsoring the plan. Can you pick from just a stock fund and a fixed-income fund, for instance, or are you offered a number of choices?

A Bank IRA

Most banks and savings and loan associations offer IRAs. In some cases, a bank will let you fund your IRA with automatic monthly deductions from your checking or savings accounts. (Again, that's an easy, relatively painless way for many people to

F.Y.I.

You can invest your IRA funds in a great many investments. That's not true of an Education IRA, however. This investment vehicle is relatively new and is not offered by every financial institution. Those firms that do offer it may limit your investment choices.

save. You never see the money, so you don't miss it.) Your credit union may let you set up an IRA, too, with automatic deductions from your paycheck.

At a bank, your IRA money will typically be invested in a money market fund or certificates of deposit (CDs). You can't move this money around as easily as other IRA investments because you may be locked into a 12-month CD. (Of course, you *can* move this money whenever you want, but you risk paying an early-withdrawal penalty.)

When an IRA CD matures, you must roll the money into another CD or a different IRA account within 60 days. If you don't, you'll owe federal tax on your interest earnings.

If you're risk averse, a bank IRA may be the right choice for you, because it's super safe. An IRA set up at a bank or savings and loan association is insured by the federal government—just like a regular savings account—up to $100,000.

A Mutual Fund IRA

Virtually every mutual fund company offers an IRA option. Under this arrangement, you can set up an IRA using any of the investments offered by that mutual fund company. In most cases, you'll have a wide variety of choices to pick from, ranging from a conservative money market fund to a growth and income fund or a balanced fund to a higher-risk agressive growth stock fund. Some investors like index funds (another option typically offered by a mutual fund company) because they're easy to understand, and they generally post better-than-average returns. (To bone up on the "basics" of mutual fund investing, see chapter 5.)

Typically, you can move your money in and out of a mutual fund—without paying federal taxes or incurring early-withdrawal penalties—as market conditions and your needs change. A mutual fund is a good choice for many IRA investors because there are so many investment options to choose from. By simply investing in a few different funds, even a novice investor can easily put together a diversified portfolio.

A Self-Directed IRA

Investors who want to manage their own portfolios may prefer the "self-directed" IRA, which offers additional investment choices. Under this arrangement, investors can buy *individual* stocks, bonds, Certificates of Deposit, and U.S. Treasury securities. With a mutual fund IRA, you can buy a stock fund; with a self-directed IRA, you can buy a particular stock.

Let's say that you set up a self-directed IRA with Vanguard. You now have the option to invest in any Vanguard mutual fund as well as mutual funds from companies other than Vanguard. In addition, you can trade individual stocks, bonds, and covered call options.

You may incur more fees with a self-directed IRA. While a bank IRA will typically cost you nothing to set up and maintain, a self-directed IRA may cost you $40 or more. You'll also have to fork over additional cash for trading fees. How much you spend will depend on how frequently you buy and sell stocks or bonds and whether you use a discount broker or a full-service broker. The transaction fees are lower for a discount broker, but you generally won't get any investment advice. A full-

F.Y.I.

You can't move a traditional IRA directly to a Roth IRA through an asset transfer. You must convert a traditional IRA to a Roth IRA, and that conversion is considered a rollover.

service broker, by contrast, will make suggestions about which stocks or bonds to buy and sell.

A self-directed IRA gives the most investment freedom, but generally it is best suited for an investor with a sizable chunk of money. You don't want to set up such an account with the first $2,000 that you're plunking into an IRA. A good time to consider this type of IRA is if you're rolling over the distribution of your 401(k) when you change jobs.

Moving Your IRA Funds

One attractive feature of an IRA is that you can move the funds in your account rather easily from one investment to another. You'll want to make such a switch if you're unhappy with your current investment's performance or if you want to change your overall investment strategy because your needs or market conditions have changed.

You can generally accomplish this movement of funds rather easily. Just pick another fund at the mutual fund company you're currently investing with, for example. If the particular investment that you want is offered by another investment firm, you'll have to do a bit more paperwork. Federal regulations permit you to transfer your IRA assets, tax-free, using two basic methods: an asset transfer or a rollover. An asset transfer is when you move your IRA funds directly from one financial institution to another. A rollover, on the other hand, is when a check is made out to you directly for the money in your IRA and you then "roll over" that check into another IRA.

The Asset Transfer

In an asset transfer, you arrange to have your IRA monies moved directly from your current custodian (T. Rowe Price, for example) to another custodian (American Century, for example). By transferring your assets in this way, you don't have to worry about incurring any early-withdrawal penalties or tax liabilities. In most cases, the new custodian will arrange this transfer for you.

The Rollover

If you withdraw the assets in your IRA before transferring them to another IRA, the transaction is called a rollover. You must deposit that money in a new IRA within 60 days. If you don't, you'll have to pay federal income tax on the money and possibly a 10 percent early-withdrawal penalty.

When you withdraw assets from your IRA, the custodian of your account is supposed to withhold 10 percent of your distribution for federal taxes—unless you tell them otherwise. In this case, if you intend to take that check and invest the money in another IRA, you generally should not have taxes withheld from your funds.

Once you've completed the rollover, you must report the transaction on your income tax return. You can't deduct a rollover contribution from your income, however, because it's not a new contribution. If you're eligible for a deductible IRA, you will have deducted that contribution in the past. (For an explanation of a deductible IRA, see chapter 3.)

You may roll over all or part of your IRA into a

F.Y.I.

You cannot treat an inherited traditional IRA as your own unless you are the decedent's surviving spouse. This means, unless the IRA investor was your husband or wife, you can't make any additional IRA contributions and you can't roll the money over. Like the original owner, however, you generally won't owe tax on the assets in the IRA until you receive distributions from it.

If you are a surviving spouse, you can use a traditional IRA inherited from your spouse as your own.

Two Ways to Move Your IRA

Thinking about moving your IRA? You can do it one of two ways: Move your IRA directly from one financial institution to another, and the transaction is called an asset transfer. Take possession of your IRA assets while transferring your account from one financial institution to another, and the transaction is called a rollover.

	In an Asset Transfer	**In a Rollover**
Your Assets . . .	Go directly from one custodian to another.	Pass into your possession between custodians.
	Remain tax-deferred with no federal tax liability.	Remain tax-deferred if redeposited in an IRA within 60 days. Otherwise, they may be subject to federal tax liability and a penalty tax for premature withdrawal.
	Can be moved as many times in a year as you wish.	Can only be moved once a year.

new IRA. (Keep in mind that you'll likely pay federal taxes and an early-withdrawal penalty on the portion of the IRA that you do not roll over.) Federal law allows only one rollover for an IRA per year. The one-year period begins on the date you receive the IRA distribution, however, not when you roll it over into the new IRA.

This rule applies to each IRA that you own. For

example, if you have two IRAs, you could roll over the assets from both of these IRAs within the same year. If you wanted to roll over the assets from a new IRA, however, you would have to wait one year to do so.

Transferring Your 401(k) Assets to Your IRA

If you're leaving your job—due to a layoff, early retirement, or a job change—you have to decide what to do with your 401(k) money. One alternative is to roll over the funds into an IRA.

As with a rollover from one IRA to another, you must roll over the assets within 60 days of receipt of the funds or you'll pay federal taxes and an early-withdrawal penalty on those funds.

What funds are eligible for a rollover? You can't roll over any after-tax contributions made to your 401(k), but you can generally roll over:

• All pretax contributions.

• Any earnings, on both pretax and after-tax contributions.

You can establish a rollover in two ways:

1. Your employer can roll over your 401(k) funds directly to the financial institution that's setting up your rollover IRA.

F.Y.I.

By rolling over your 401(k) distribution into an IRA, you can:

• Avoid current income taxes and any early-withdrawal penalty.

• Keep your money growing tax-deferred.

2. Your employer can draft a check, payable to the financial institution that's setting up your rollover IRA.

There is a third option, but for reasons you'll soon understand, you don't want to take it. If your 401(k) distribution is made payable to *you* (that's option number 3), your employer must withhold 20 percent of your distribution for prepayment of your federal income taxes. This applies even if you plan to roll over the distribution into an IRA.

You'll have to replace the 20 percent that was withheld by your employer with your own money within 60 days of receiving your distribution, or that 20 percent will be treated as a taxable distribution and you may be subject to an additional 10 percent early-withdrawal penalty if you're younger than age 59½. (You'll get that 20 percent paid in withholding tax back *eventually,* but only after you file your tax return and wait for your refund.)

When you establish a rollover IRA with your 401(k) assets, it's best not to mix this money with any regular IRA contributions. Keep this IRA separate. How come? You may get another job in the future that offers a 401(k). To consolidate your retirement assets into one account, you could roll this IRA back into a 401(k). You won't be permitted to do that, however, if you've commingled the assets with other IRA contributions.

You can roll over all or a portion of your 401(k) distribution. If you need to tap into the money in the near future, you may want to roll over the entire amount (if you can wait that long for the cash) and simply make a withdrawal from your IRA at a later date. Withdrawals from a rollover IRA aren't subject to the 20 percent withholding that applies to distributions from a 401(k) plan. IRA withdrawals are subject to current income taxes, however, as well as a 10 percent IRS early-withdrawal penalty if you're younger than age 59½.

Consider Your Asset Allocation

When you began contributing to your 401(k) plan, you had to decide how to invest those contributions. Most likely, you didn't plunk all of your retirement savings into a single investment. You allocated your investment money to different asset classes, depending upon your risk tolerance, your age, your investment time horizon, and other factors. (For a complete discussion of asset allocation, see chapter 6.)

If you're leaving your current employer, however, due to a layoff, a career change, or early retirement, you're probably experiencing some major life changes. As a result, your ability to withstand risk may have changed significantly, so your asset allocation strategy may no longer be appropriate.

As you select the investments that you'd like to roll your 401(k) distribution into, consider your new status and readjust your asset allocation accordingly. For instance, if you've left your job because you accepted an early-retirement package, you may want to take less risk with your investments. This is especially true if you were planning on working another 10 years or so but now are unsure what you'll do in the future. On the other hand, if you've accepted a higher-paying job at a top-notch company, you may feel as though you want to take on more risk.

The investments you choose for your IRA rollover will also depend on your time horizon. Will you need to dip into this account in the near future? If so, consider investing some of the rollover into a short-term investment such as a Certificate of Deposit or a money market account.

An important point to bear in mind: No matter what investments you choose for your IRA rollover today, you can always reallocate those assets to different investments in the future. With an IRA, you're not locked into any investment forever. Your Individual Retirement Account, remember, is merely a tax sheltered account that lets your money grow tax-deferred. You need to invest that account in the investments of your choice.

THE BOTTOM LINE

Investing in an IRA is just like investing in a 401(k) plan. You're responsible for making your own decisions about which investments to put your savings into. The main difference? With an IRA, you can invest in almost any stock, bond, or fund. With a 401(k), you're limited to the investment choices offered by your employer.

The rewards of tax-deferred investing can still be yours—even if you leave your job and must take your 401(k) savings with you. Roll over those funds into an Individual Retirement Account within 60 days of disbursement of the funds and the transaction will be tax-free. Your savings will continue to grow tax-deferred, too.

Taking Your Money Out of Your 401(k)

A 401(k) plan is designed to help you save money. At some point, however, you'll have to take money out of your account. Perhaps you're only 45—and not even close to retirement age—but you need your 401(k) funds to help pay your medical bills or avoid foreclosure on your home. Maybe you'd like to simply borrow some of your 401(k) assets to renovate your house or pay for your son's college tuition. Or you may be 65 (and recently retired) and need the money to help pay expenses. Or you might've just turned 70½ years of age and you're required by law to withdraw some of the cash. No matter what your age or circumstances, there are several ways to tap into your 401(k) account.

All withdrawals and loans are subject to certain taxes. If you withdraw the money before age 59½, you may be charged a 10 percent early-withdrawal penalty (in addition to regular income taxes). Many plans let you borrow money from your account, but not all do. Your Summary Plan Description should outline the types of withdrawals and loans permitted in your plan. The various withdrawal options available in many plans are discussed in this chapter.

Taking Your Money Out Before Retirement

In a perfect world, your 401(k) savings would remain untouched until retirement. But life is unpredictable and you may need to tap into that money sooner. There are a few ways that you are generally permitted to do this. You may withdraw money from your account for a "financial hardship," such as the purchase of a new home or the cost of your child's college tuition. You may also withdraw money if you become disabled and for other "special" circumstances. Finally, some plans let you borrow money against your account for any reason.

The Hardship Withdrawal

The IRS lets you withdraw money from your 401(k) for "immediate and heavy financial need." These needs, which you must not be able to meet by any other means, include the following:

• Unreimbursed medical expenses for you or your dependents. These expenses must exceed 7.5 percent of your adjusted gross income.

• Purchase of your principal residence. That's the home you live in. A vacation home doesn't qualify.

• College tuition—for you, your spouse, or one of your dependents.

• Amount needed to prevent foreclosure or eviction from your home.

You must prove "need." You may have to include copies of your medical bills, for instance, or your son's tuition bills with your request for a hardship withdrawal. Generally, your plan should ex-

F.Y.I.

If you are married, you must get the written consent of your spouse, witnessed by either a notary or a plan representative, for a hardship withdrawal.

plain what financial need is in its Summary Plan Description.

You can't withdraw more money than you need. That's a bit more than it appears, though. Generally, you can take enough to cover taxes and penalties related to the hardship withdrawal, too. In the end, you should have the exact amount needed for the hardship and the taxes and penalties.

Although some plans stipulate that only employee contributions—and not matching dollars or earnings on the contributions—can be withdrawn, you can typically withdraw the following:

- Rollover contributions

- Salary deferral contributions

- Any vested matching contributions

Unlike a loan, however, a hardship withdrawal needn't be paid back. But you will be expected to pay certain taxes and penalties. Generally, hardship withdrawals are subject to ordinary income taxes and, if you're under age 59½, a 10 percent early-withdrawal penalty.

If you make a hardship withdrawal, you usually can't make additional contributions to your 401(k) for a period of time (often a year from the date of the hardship withdrawal). In addition, the total amount that you can contribute to your plan from your salary in the following tax year will be reduced by the amount that you contributed the year that you took the hardship withdrawal.

For example: You defer $2,000 into your plan from January 1 to July 1, 1999. You take a hardship withdrawal on July 1, 1999. You are not permitted to make any further contributions until July 1, 2000. From July 1 to December 31, 2000, your contributions will be limited to $8,000 because you contributed $2,000 the year before and the maximum deferral amount permitted for that year is $10,000:

Maximum Deferral Amount
Permitted in 2000 $10,000

Less the Amount Deferred
in 1999 $2,000

Maximum Amount Allowed
to Contribute in 2000 $8,000

Withdrawals Under Special Circumstances

You or your heirs can withdraw your 401(k) funds penalty-free—even if you're under age 59½—for the following reasons:

1. You've incurred substantial medical expenses. If you tap into your 401(k) to pay medical expenses for yourself, your spouse, or your dependents, you may not have to pay that 10 percent early-withdrawal penalty on all of the funds withdrawn. This "circumstance" is somewhat complicated, but in general you don't have to pay a penalty for 401(k) funds withdrawn that are used to pay for medical expenses that would be deductible if you itemized deductions on your tax return. (You don't have to itemize to take advantage of this exemption.)

Note, however, that your medical expenses are

SMART MONEY

"If you should die, any money in a 401(k) plan, including all employer contributions, will go to your named beneficiary. If that person is your spouse, he or she will have the same options [that you have]. A beneficiary who is not your spouse will not have the rollover option. Instead, such a beneficiary will have to take the money, either in a lump sum or over a period of years not to exceed his or her life expectancy (as determined by IRS regulations)."

Source: Life Advice Pamphlet About 401(k) Plans. Reproduced with permission of the MetLife Consumer Education Company.

not 100 percent deductible. According to the IRS, only those medical expenses that exceed 7.5 percent of your adjusted gross income are deductible. For example: You had $7,000 in medical expenses last year, and your adjusted gross income was $75,000. What portion of your your medical expenses are deductible? $1,375.

(Here's how it's calculated: 7.5% of $75,000 is $5,625. $7,000 – $5,625 = $1,375.)

If you withdrew that $7,000 from your 401(k), you wouldn't have to pay a penalty on $1,375 of it. The remainder of your withdrawal would be subject to penalty, though. And you must pay income tax on the whole withdrawal amount of $7,000.

2. You have become permanently disabled. What qualifies as a "disability" will be defined by your specific plan. In general, though, you must be unable to return to work (and thus support yourself) for the foreseeable future. One bright spot: Many plans consider you "fully vested" as soon as you become disabled even if you haven't yet actually fulfilled the vesting time requirements.

3. You die. Your heirs can withdraw the money from your plan without incurring that 10 percent early-withdrawal penalty. Who gets the money? The person named as the beneficiary. If you're married, that's probably your spouse. He or she can roll the money into an IRA and continue to defer taxes on your investment. Your spouse can also withdraw the money and spend it if he or she wishes. But, of course, income taxes will be due on such a withdrawal.

4. You are at least 55 years old, and you were laid off, fired, quit your job, or took early retirement. This loophole applies only to 401(k) plans. It does not apply to Individual Retirement Accounts. Nor does it apply to folks who qualify for early retirement at their jobs at age 52 or 54 and wait until they turn 55 to start taking distributions from their plan. No matter what your employer's policy on early retirement, you must be age 55 or older *when you leave your job* to avoid paying the penalty for early withdrawal.

Borrowing from Your 401(k)

Many 401(k) plans let you borrow money from your account. In the past, companies often asked why you wanted to borrow the funds. It had to be deemed an "emergency" or the loan wouldn't be permitted. Nowadays, many companies will let you borrow money for any reason.

By law, you can borrow up to 50 percent of your account's vested assets, or $50,000, whichever is less. If you have $50,000 in your account, for example, and you're fully vested, you can borrow up to $25,000.

Typically you can have only one loan outstanding at a time, and you can take out a loan just once in a twelve-month period.

No taxes or early-withdrawal penalties would be incurred with such a loan, unless you didn't pay the money back.

Repayment of the principal (the borrowed amount) plus interest are made to your account through payroll deductions. Generally, these re-payments start immediately and must be paid in full within five years. If you use the borrowed funds to buy a home, however, which you plan to use as your primary residence, you can frequently take as long as 20 to 30 years to repay the loan.

As with any loan, there are advantages and dis-advantages to this method of borrowing. On the positive side, a loan from your 401(k) account means:

1. You repay yourself—with interest. Since you're essentially borrowing your own money, you pay yourself back rather than a bank or other lender.

2. You'll probably get an attractive interest rate. The interest rate on such loans is generally deter-mined by the plan administrator and is usually prime plus one or two percentage points. In most cases, that's less than what most banks would charge you for a similar loan.

3. You can get the money quickly. Often, you can get a loan from your 401(k) account simply by call-ing your company's benefits office or the 800 num-ber listed in your Summary Plan Description. If your plan allows loans by phone, you'll get a check within a few days. Even if you must fill out a form to request a loan, a check should arrive within two weeks. Since you are borrowing your own money, a credit check is not required.

There are some drawbacks. A loan from your 401(k) account could mean that:

1. You have to repay the loan—immediately. If you leave the company or are laid off while your

Borrowing from Your 401(k): Is It Worth It?

A loan from your 401(k) may not be your smartest borrowing option. If you own your own home, for instance, you may be able to take out a home equity loan instead. The advantage of this borrowing option is that the interest paid on a home equity loan is tax-deductible. (It is not tax-deductible on a 401(k) loan, however.)

Even if the interest rate on your home equity loan is higher than the rate charged on your 401(k) loan, the home equity loan may actually cost you less because the interest is tax-deductible. The drawback with a home equity loan, of course, is that you're using your house as collateral for your loan. If you default on your payments, you could lose your home.

To figure out which loan better meets your needs, fill out this worksheet designed by David Godofsky, principal at Bryan, Pendleton, Swats & McAllister, an employee-benefits consulting firm in Nashville, Tennessee.

1. Enter your marginal tax rate. _____

2. Subtract line 1 from 100 percent. _____

3. Enter the annual percentage rate (APR) you would pay for a home equity loan. _____

4. Multiply line 2 by line 3. This is your after-tax cost of borrowing. _____

5. Enter the rate you expect to earn on your 401(k) investment. _____

If line 4 is greater than line 5, borrow from your 401(k). If line 5 is greater than line 4, take the home equity loan.

Source: Originally appeared in *Money* magazine, September 1995.

F.Y.I.

Loan payments made to your 401(k) are not tax-deductible—even if you're using the borrowed funds to buy a home. The reasoning? You already got a tax break when you put your money into the account, pre-tax. The IRS doesn't allow two tax breaks for the same money.

loan is still outstanding, you'll be expected to repay the amount that you still owe, within 30 days. If you can't come up with the cash, the loan will be considered a withdrawal. You must then pay federal income tax on the loan amount that's outstanding, and, if you're under age 59½, you'll incur a 10 percent early-withdrawal penalty.

2. You have to pay to borrow your own money. Some 401(k) plans charge a fee to set up and maintain your loan, just as a bank would do. Under some plans, you'll be charged a one-time loan-initiation fee and an annual processing fee.

3. You're depleting your retirement nest egg. While it's true that you are paying interest back to yourself, you're probably not earning as much as you would if you had left the money untouched in your account. For example: Let's assume that your account is earning 12 percent. You are paying 8 percent interest on your borrowed funds. The result? You're losing 4 percent. What's more, you're paying that interest with after-tax dollars, whereas your account is earning its return from the pre-tax dollars already invested in your account.

Look at the three examples in the box on the next page. Borrowing from your 401(k) account can affect the amount of money available at retirement.

In the examples shown, Smith has $19,590 more than Jones and $256,781 more than Rogers at retirement because he did not borrow funds from his 401(k) account. Although both Jones and Rogers borrowed money from their 401(k) plans, Jones has $237,191 more than Rogers because he kept making contributions even when his loan was outstanding.

How a 401(k) Can Affect Your Retirement Savings

Can a 401(k) loan significantly affect your retirement nest egg? That depends if you continue to make contributions while your loan is outstanding. In this example, Smith never taps into his 401(k) account. Jones takes advantage of his plan's loan feature but continues to make contributions even while his loan is outstanding. Rogers takes out a loan, too, but unlike Jones, she doesn't make any contributions (in addition to the repayment of the principal and interest to her account) while her loan is outstanding:

Smith	**Jones**	**Rogers**
Contributes for 30 years. *No Loan*	Contributes for 30 years. *$15,000 Loan*	Contributes but stops for 5 years until loan is repaid. *$15,000 Loan*
Balance at age 35:		
$ 5,000	$ 5,000	$ 5,000
Balance at age 39:		
$ 32,052	$ 16,302	$ 16,302
Balance at age 44:		
$ 83,671	$ 81,024	$ 48,972
Balance at age 55:		
$336,013	$328,460	$237,013
Balance at age 65:		
$955,203	$935,613	$698,422

The above example assumes the following: $5,000/year contribution (10 percent of $50,000 annual salary); investment return of 10 percent; loan interest rate of 7 percent (compounded monthly) on a 5-year loan; borrowed $15,000, starting in year 5.

Source: David Godofsky, principal, Bryan, Pendleton, Swats & McAllister, Nashville, Tennessee.

At first glance, those numbers seem contradictory. Smith's and Jones's balances are rather close—even though Smith didn't borrow. And Jones's and Rogers's balances are rather disparate—even though they both took out loans.

Their stories neatly illustrate the advantages and the drawbacks of 401(k) loans, however. Rogers is clearly the loser because he stopped making contributions—even though it was for a short period of time—and thus lost the opportunity for additional money to grow tax-deferred for 25 years.

Jones, on the other hand, doesn't lose nearly as much ground, even though he tapped into his account, too. Consider: His 401(k) account was earning 10 percent interest on the money he borrowed. He was charged 7 percent to borrow that money. Since he pays the principal and interest back into his account, Jones is essentially losing 3 percent interest (10 percent – 7 percent) during the term of the loan. As a result, his retirement balance is just about $20,000 less than Smith's balance. Or so it seems. In reality, though, Jones is losing more than that. That 7 percent interest his 401(k) is earning during his loan period is coming out of his own pocket (and thus cutting into his discretionary income that could be invested elsewhere) rather than from the fund itself. Thus, his 401(k) isn't really earning *any* money in the market at all, in fact, during the period his loan is outstanding.

A 401(k) loan probably makes the most sense if you really need to borrow the money and you have no other loan options available. Obviously, it's a smarter idea to *borrow* your 401(k) funds than to merely *withdraw* them because in the latter case you'll have to pay income taxes and an early-withdrawal penalty. With a 401(k) loan, you can get the money that you need and still save for retirement—but at a somewhat slower rate.

What Happens When You Leave Your Current Job?

A 401(k) plan is portable. That means you can take your money with you should you change jobs or get fired. What exactly should you do with the money in your retirement plan? You *could* spend it all on a round-the-world trip, but you have several, more prudent options to choose from, too.

Leave Your 401(k) Savings in Your Former Employer's Plan

If you have at least $5,000 invested in your former employer's plan, you generally can just leave it there—even though you no longer work for the company. This alternative lets your money continue to grow tax-deferred, and it doesn't subject you to any current income taxes or IRS penalties. However, you cannot continue to contribute money to the plan nor can you borrow money from it.

By leaving your money in the plan, you may find that your options are limited in other ways, too, such as:

SMART MONEY

"Once you leave your company, no one wants to deal with you because you don't work there anymore. You call up to find out some information about your 401(k) and it's almost impossible to get a human voice on the phone," says Ed Slott, a certified public accountant in Rockville Center, New York, and the author of *Ed Slott's IRA Advisor*, a monthly newsletter (800-663-1340) that discusses tax protection of your retirement assets. "You're almost always better off rolling your money into an IRA."

- **Withdrawals are stricter.** You may not be able to take any money out of the plan until you retire or reach a certain age.

- **Your investment options have shrunk.** Since you no longer work for the company, you may not be offered all the investment options anymore. Or you may not be able to move from one investment option to another as often as you did in the past.

- **Additional fees are charged.** Because you are now an ex-employee, you may be charged for services that you used to get for free.

Take the Money Out of Your Account—In Cash

You can withdraw all of the money and spend it on that dream vacation. But you'll have less money for retirement, and it'll cost you now in taxes and, if you're under 55, penalties. You'll probably end up with far less than you were expecting.

For example: Let's assume that you expect to receive $15,000. Your employer is required by the IRS to withhold 20 percent of your distribution for prepayment of federal income taxes. That means you're getting a check for $12,000; the other $3,000 is going to the government for taxes. Next, you'll have to pay ordinary income taxes on the entire $15,000 amount (even though you never actually received that amount). Depending on your tax bracket, that could mean you may have to pay more than the 20 percent already withheld. (In this case, you'd have to pay Federal income taxes of $2,400.)

In addition, you may have to pay another 10 percent in penalties for withdrawing the money prematurely. If you withdraw the money when you're age 55 or older, though, you won't incur the 10 percent penalty. (See "Withdrawals under Special Circumstances," page 167.)

How Taxes and Penalties Could Drain Your Distribution

	Example	Your Calculation
1. Eligible retirement plan distribution	$15,000	$ _____
2. 20% withholding required (for prepayment of federal income tax)	– $3,000	$ _____
3. Additional federal income tax (multipy line 1 by .16 for 36% tax bracket; .08 for 28% tax bracket)	– $2,400	$ _____
4. 10% early withdrawal penalty (if younger than age 59½)[1]	– $1,500	$ _____
Amount left to spend or reinvest	$8,100	$ _____

1. If you are at least age 55 and terminating employment, the 10 percent early-withdrawal penalty may not apply.

Source: Fidelity Investments. Copyright 1998 FMR Corp. All rights reserved. Reprinted by permission.

SMART SOURCES

IRAs, 401(k)s, and Other Retirement Plans: Taking Your Money Out, by Twila Slesnick, Ph.D., Enrolled Agent, and Attorney John C. Suttle, CPA, answers every conceivable question regarding penalties, taxes, and distributions from your 401(k) and IRA.

Transfer the Funds to a New Employer's Plan

Not all employers will accept money from a previous 401(k) plan, but many do. You may have to wait a year to become eligible, however, to participate in your new employer's plan. At that time, you could roll over your old 401(k) into your new plan. If that's the case, you may want to leave your plan with your former employer or roll it over into an IRA. (See "Roll Over the Money into an IRA" below.)

When you transfer funds from one plan to another, make sure that you transfer the money directly. This way, you'll avoid the 20 percent withholding tax and the 10 percent early-withdrawal penalty.

Roll Over the Money into an IRA

To avoid paying current income taxes and an early-withdrawal penalty, you can roll over your 401(k) assets into an IRA. As with the transfer of money to another employer's plan, make sure that the money is transferred directly from one institution to another so that you avoid having taxes withheld.

At this point, you may want to consider a Roth IRA instead of a traditional IRA. While you can't convert assets from an employer's retirement plan directly to a Roth IRA, you can roll over an eligible distribution to a traditional IRA and then pay the taxes and convert that IRA to a Roth.

Is it a good idea, taxwise? The situation is the

same as if you were deciding whether to convert an existing IRA to a Roth IRA. Your money will continue to grow tax-deferred, and you can continue to make contributions as long as you have earned income. (With a traditional IRA, you can't make contributions after age 70½.) The other main advantages: Withdrawals from the account are completely tax-free, and you don't have to take a certain amount out of your account each year because there is no mandatory withdrawal schedule. (For a fuller discussion of the Roth IRA and IRA rollovers, see chapters 3 and 7, respectively.)

Withdrawing the Money at Retirement

You've decided to retire. Now is the time to reap the benefits of your 401(k) savings. You can withdraw all of the money in your 401(k) account in one lump-sum distribution. (You'll pay the taxes due on that money all at once, too.) Or you can take your money out of your account more gradually, in installment payments each year. (Your tax bill will be similarly stretched out over time.) Whatever method of payment you select, you must adhere to certain rules, set by the IRS, about when, and how much, you must withdraw from your plan.

Required Withdrawals

Once you turn 70½ years old and are retired, the IRS says that you must withdraw a minimum amount from your 401(k) account each year.

F.Y.I.

If you declare bankruptcy, the money in your 401(k) can't be touched by your creditors. But the money in your IRA can. That's one good reason to consider leaving your 401(k) with your employer after you retire and take the money out in installments rather than a lump-sum payment, which you then roll over into an IRA.

(Technically, you have until April 1 of the year after you turn 70½.) If you're not yet retired at this age, some plans require that you begin taking the minimum amount out anyway. Other plans let you defer payments until you retire. The IRS, however, requires that you begin taking distributions by April 1 of the year after you retire.

If you don't withdraw the minimum amount in time (or if you don't take enough), you'll pay a penalty. And it's a doozy: a whopping 50 percent on the amount that you should have withdrawn. If you didn't withdraw enough, you'll pay a 50 percent penalty on the difference between the amount that was withdrawn and the amount that should have been withdrawn. (Obviously, taxes are due when you withdraw any money from a 401(k) plan.)

How Much Must You Withdraw?

The amount is based on your life expectancy. The IRS publishes various tables, which list the life expectancy of married and single people at different ages. (See "Single Life Expectancies" on the next page.) Basically, your 401(k) account balance is divided by a life expectancy to determine your required distribution. For instance, the IRS says that at age 71 your life expectancy divisor is 15.3. Therefore, your account balance of $2.5 million, for example, would be divided by 15.3. Your minimum withdrawal for the year would be $163,398.69.

If you want to reduce your required withdrawals (and still adhere to IRS requirements), consider recalculating your life expectancy each

Single Life Expectancies

Age	Divisor	Age	Divisor
50	33.1	76	11.9
51	32.2	77	11.2
52	31.3	78	10.6
53	30.4	79	10.0
54	29.5	80	9.5
55	28.6	81	8.9
56	27.7	82	8.4
57	26.8	83	7.9
58	25.9	84	7.4
59	25.0	85	6.9
60	24.2	86	6.5
61	23.3	87	6.1
62	22.5	88	5.7
63	21.6	89	5.3
64	20.8	90	5.0
65	20.0	91	4.7
66	19.2	92	4.4
67	18.4	93	4.1
68	17.6	94	3.9
69	16.8	95	3.7
70	16.0	96	3.4
71	15.3	97	3.2
72	14.6	98	3.0
73	13.9	99	2.8
74	13.2	100	2.7
75	12.5		

Source: Internal Revenue Service, Publication 939.

year. (You'll need an accountant or some other financial adviser to do this for you.) Your minimum withdrawal amount will be slightly less in the early years of your retirement if you refigure the numbers every year rather than just once at the onset of retirement. (The calculation for this fixed payout set up front is called term certain.) If you're married, you may also be able to reduce your required withdrawals by using the joint life expectancy table (from the IRS) rather than a single life expectancy figure for you alone.

Calculating the Withdrawal Amount

There are two methods used to calculate the minimum withdrawal from a 401(k):

Term Certain

The balance of your 401(k) account is divided by your life expectancy (either yours alone or the combined life expectancy of you and your spouse), as determined by an actuarial table. The annual distribution rate of your funds is established upon your retirement and will continue to be paid at that rate until your 401(k) funds are depleted.

Recalculation Method

As with the "term certain" method, the balance of your 401(k) account is similarly divided by your life expectancy. In this case, however, your life expectancy is recalculated each year (rather than once). The annual distribution rate of your funds is based on these new calculations each year.

The benefit of this method is that you're generally required to withdraw less in the early years of your retirement (leaving more money to be paid over a longer period of time). The major drawback of the recalculation method is tax related. When one spouse dies, the other spouse must take a larger minimum distribution each year (and pay tax on it). Similarly, when both spouses die, the remaining assets go to the estate and are taxed in full.

How to Take the Money Out

At retirement, you can take your money out of your 401(k) plan in several ways. You can withdraw the money out all at once, for instance, or you can simply take the money out as you need it. It's up to you.

The basic withdrawal options are discussed below. But because these choices may be more complicated than they appear (depending upon your particular tax situation) and because some of these choices are irreversible, it is often recommended that you get professional guidance from an accountant, a certified financial planner, or another financial adviser before making a decision.

Take a Lump-Sum Payment

With this setup, you get all the money all at once. That's great if you need the money to finance your retirement fantasy of traveling around the world or some other dream that requires a sizable chunk of ready cash. Trouble is, when you withdraw your 401(k) balance in one lump sum, your money stops growing tax-deferred and you must pay all the taxes due on this money at once. In addition, your decision is irreversible.

You may be able to save some money on taxes, however, if you're eligible for an IRS tax break known as "forward averaging." Your taxes are reduced using this method because they are "averaged" as though you had withdrawn your money over a 5- or 10-year period. Why is the IRS so generous? Because they're getting your money now, rather than receiving annual payments over the next 20 or 30 years. (This tax break does not apply to 403(b) accounts, however.)

Roll Over the Money into an IRA

The smartest alternative for a lump sum 401(k) distribution at retirement generally is, once again, to roll over the money to an IRA. Have you tired of hearing this advice yet? The truth is, an IRA rollover, in most instances, gives you the most control—and the most flexibility—in terms of investment and estate-planning options.

With an IRA rollover, you have a wide choice of investment options. You can invest in just about any stock, bond, or fund that you choose. If you were to leave the money with your employer and take payments, for instance (see those sections on the following pages), you would be limited to the investment choices offered through the plan by your employer.

In addition, your estate planning options will

be more limited, in most cases, also. IRAs typically have more flexible beneficiary distribution rules than 401(k)s. For example: By the time you retire (assuming you've been saving money in your 401(k) regularly), you may well have accumulated a portfolio worth $400,000 or more. How are you going to leave that to your heirs—without causing them to lose a significant portion of the money in estate taxes?

Let's say, for instance, that you want to designate your child as the beneficiary. Generally, you can do that if you leave the money with your employer and receive periodic payments. But most 401(k) plans don't continue to make payments to children after the death of the beneficiary. Often, they'll pay the child the entire balance, and your child will then have to pay substantial estate taxes on that lump sum payment.

With an IRA rollover, by contrast, you can still name your child as the beneficiary. The difference is, though, you call the shots. You can develop an estate planning strategy (with the help of a tax specialist or a financial planner) that can bypass some of that tax by paying the balance to your child using the term method. Your child will then receive the money in installments over a term of years, which generally reduces the amount of tax due.

Finally, if you choose an IRA rollover, you also have the option of paying the taxes on the rollover and converting it to a Roth IRA. Why would you do that? Your withdrawals will then be completely tax-free, and you don't have to take any mandatory withdrawals—ever. (See chapter 7 for a more complete discussion of IRA rollovers.)

What Matters

• You can tap into your 401(k) account if you're hard pressed for funds. You may qualify for a hardship withdrawal or, under many plans, you may borrow money from your account.

• Once you turn 70½ years old and are retired, you must withdraw a minimum amount each year from your 401(k).

What Doesn't

• It's not an emergency. But you want to borrow from your 401(k) plan, anyway. Nowadays, companies will often let you borrow money from your account for any reason.

• You're 55 years old and you're withdrawing your money prematurely. You won't incur a penalty—if you were laid off, fired, quit your job, or took early retirement.

Buy an Annuity

An annuity pays a fixed amount monthly for life—that's your life or the life of your beneficiary. Your employer may pay your retirement plan benefits in the form of an annuity. You can also arrange this setup yourself by rolling your account balance into an IRA and using the money to buy an annuity from a life insurance company.

Annuites offer several payout options. A "straight life annuity" option, for instance, will make monthly payments for your lifetime—no matter how long you live. The drawback: Should you die young, the insurance company keeps the balance of your account. A "joint and survivor" option, common for married couples, pays an income to you and your spouse for life. If you die before your spouse, the annuity still pays him or her, but the payments are lower (they could be as much as 50 percent less). A life annuity with a "term certain" option guarantees that you'll receive a "certain" number of payments, whether you're alive or not. A life annuity with a "five-year period certain," for instance, is paid to you for life. If you don't live past your term (five years, in this example), your beneficiary will receive the remaining payments.

The benefits of an annuity are that you receive a fixed amount for life, and there's no work involved. You just collect your check every month. That's appealing to some retirees. But you give up control of your investments for that stability. And your heirs don't get all of your account balance when you die.

Leave the Money in Your Plan and Receive Regular Installment Payments

Your employer may let you leave your money in the company plan, even after you've retired. That lets your money continue to grow tax-deferred, until you need it. The IRS requires you to take a minimum amount per year, which you can typically arrange through installment payments.

Some plans let you take the money in annual installments; others let you receive payments on a monthly, quarterly, semiannual, or annual basis. Taxes are due annually, however, on the money you withdrew during the year.

One drawback with this type of disbursement: Your investment choices are limited to those options offered by your employer's plan. If you rolled the money over into an IRA, for instance, you would have a greater variey of investment options to pick from as well as more flexibile estate-planning options.

Leave the Money in Your Plan and Take Occasional Payments

Some companies let you withdraw money from your 401(k) account whenever you like, as often as you like. The amount that you withdraw is up to you also, but you must withdraw the minimum amount required each year by the IRS.

Should you die before you've taken all of the

THE BOTTOM LINE

A 401(k) plan is a long-term savings plan. At some point, though, you'll want to start dipping into that cash.

You may have to tap into those funds in an emergency, for instance, long before you're eligible for retirement. If you're younger than age 59½, you'll pay a 10 percent penalty for withdrawing your savings early—unless you qualify for a hardship withdrawal.

If it's a loan that you want, you can, under many plans, borrow your own funds. You'll pay this money back, with interest, to your account.

Once you're ready to retire, you can withdraw your money as a lump-sum distribution and roll it over into an IRA or leave it with your employer and make periodic withdrawals. By age 70½, you generally must begin making minimum withdrawals.

money out of your account, the balance is generally paid to your beneficiary in one lump-sum payment.

Again, the drawback with this arrangement is that your investment choices are limited to those options offered by your employer's plan. You would have a greater variety of investment options if you rolled the money into an IRA as well as more flexible estate-planning options.

....

Taking Your Money Out of Your IRA

An Individual Retirement Account (IRA) is a savings plan that lets you save money, tax-deferred, for retirement. At some point, you'll want—or need—to take some of this money out to pay for living expenses, to stash in another investment, or to buy that boat you've always dreamed of. Whether your IRA represents the core of your retirement savings or merely supplements the savings you have invested in your 401(k) or a similar defined-contribution plan, you can't just tap into this account at whim. There are rules limiting the withdrawal and use of your IRA assets.

If you break these rules, you'll generally have to pay additional taxes. How much you'll pay will depend upon when you make your withdrawals, why you're withdrawing the money, and what type of IRA you have invested in: a traditional IRA, a Roth IRA, or an Education IRA.

The Traditional IRA

An Individual Retirement Account (IRA) is a savings plan that lets you put aside money for your retirement. Your contributions grow tax-deferred until you withdraw the funds at retirement. Unlike a 401(k) plan, an IRA is not offered by your employer. It is a retirement savings account that you may set up yourself at a bank, a mutual fund company, or a brokerage firm. Funds in an IRA may be invested in a variety of investments, including stocks and bonds. Each year, you can contribute up to $2,000, and, depending upon certain criteria, you may be able to deduct all or a portion of your contribution on your income tax return.

The 10 Percent Early-Withdrawal Penalty

When you put money into an IRA, your annual contributions and the earnings grow tax-deferred. In exchange for that tax benefit, you must keep your money in the account until you are at least 59½ years old. If you withdraw the money from your account before that time, you'll be charged a 10 percent penalty for early withdrawal.

Take George, for example. He is 38 years old. Every year he puts the maximum $2,000 allowed into his IRA, which he deducts on his income taxes. This year, he withdraws $5,000 from his account to buy a used car. Because George is not yet 59½ years old, his withdrawal is considered "premature." As a result, he must pay the 10 percent penalty. In this case, George will pay $500 to the IRS (10 percent x $5,000), plus the income taxes owed, as explained below.

Income Taxes Due

Regardless of your age—or the reason that you're withdrawing your funds—when you withdraw money from a traditional IRA, you must pay income tax on your account's earnings and on any contributions for which you took a deduction on your income taxes. Using the above example, 38-year-old George will have to pay income tax on the amount withdrawn. This would be true whenever he withdrew the money. Had George withdrawn the money when he was older, he might pay less in taxes because at that point he might be in a lower tax bracket.

Because George made only *tax-deductible* contributions to this IRA, however, he must pay income tax on both his contributions and the earnings when he withdraws the money from his account. (This amount is charged in addition to the 10 percent early-withdrawal penalty.)

If you make *nondeductible* contributions to your IRA, however, you don't owe any tax when you withdraw those contributions. Why? Because you already paid income tax on that money before you invested it in your IRA. If you paid income tax on those contributions at withdrawal, you'd be paying tax twice on the same money. You will owe taxes on any *earnings*, however, that are withdrawn from your account.

Suppose you made both deductible and nondeductible contributions over the years? That's a bit trickier. You only owe taxes on the contributions that were deductible. To calculate this tax amount, you must complete IRS Form 8606, which helps you figure out how much of your IRA withdrawal is taxable in any given year.

Withdrawing Those IRA Assets Early—Without Penalty

You must pay a 10 percent penalty if you withdraw assets from your IRA before you reach age 59½. That's the general rule. The IRS allows some exceptions, though, which may help you out in times of your or your family's financial hardship:

• **Your death.** If you die before reaching age 59½, the assets in your traditional IRA will go to your beneficiary (or your estate, as the case may be) and will not be subject to the 10 percent early-withdrawal penalty.

• **You become disabled.** If you become disabled before age 59½, any money that you withdraw from your IRA won't be subject to the 10 percent early-withdrawal penalty. Disability, as defined by the IRS, means that "you cannot do any substantial gainful activity because of your physical or mental condition." A note from your physician outlining the length and degree of your disability is required.

• **Payment of medical insurance premiums.** You may not have to pay the 10 percent for the early withdrawal if you use the money withdrawn to pay for medical insurance for yourself, your spouse, and your dependents. The catch? You must have lost your job and received unemployment for more than 12 weeks.

• **Unreimbursed medical expenses.** Even if you're under age 59½, you don't have to pay the 10 percent early-withdrawal penalty if you use the money to pay significant unreimbursed medical expenses. However, you can only take into account medical expenses that you would be able to deduct on your income taxes. In general, you can deduct only those unreimbursed expenses that exceed 7.5 percent of your adjusted gross income. (You don't have to itemize your deductions, however, to take advantage of this exception.)

• **First-time home purchase.** You can withdraw up to $10,000 to help you, your spouse, your children, even your grandchildren buy a new home. If both you and your spouse are first-time home buyers, you can each withdraw up to $10,000, penalty-free, for a combined total of $20,000.

• **Higher-education expenses.** You can withdraw money, penalty-free, to help yourself and those same family members listed above pay for college or other post-secondary education expenses such as tuition, books, supplies, and equipment.

• **Equal withdrawals made over a certain time period.** Even if you're not yet age 59½, you can withdraw funds penalty-free if you take the money as "a series of substantially equal payments" over your life expectancy or the joint life expectancy of you and your spouse. For the exception to apply, however, you must take at least one payment annually for at least five years, or until you reach age 59½ (whichever is the longer period).

Withdrawing Your Traditional IRA Assets at Retirement

Once you turn 59½, you can begin to make withdrawals from your traditional IRA, penalty-free. But you don't have to. If you take the money out between age 59½ and age 70½, there are no limitations as to how much money, or how little, you must withdraw from your IRA.

You can continue to make contributions to your account, in fact, until you reach age 70½. At that time, you cannot make any further contributions, even if you are still working. For many folks, it makes sense to keep pumping money into an IRA for as long as possible. Your investment continues to grow tax-deferred, and if you need some quick cash, you can now dip into your account, penalty-free, as often as you need to. You can make withdrawals and contributions in the same year.

Required Withdrawals

"You cannot keep funds in a traditional IRA indefinitely. Eventually you *must* withdraw them." That's the law, according to the IRS. By April 1 of the year after you reach age 70½, you must begin making withdrawals from your account—even if you are still working.

If you don't make the required withdrawals, or if you don't withdraw enough money in a given year, you may have to pay a 50 percent excise tax on the required amount that was not withdrawn.

Okay, but . . . how much do you have to withdraw? You must take out enough money each year so that your entire account will be used up over your life expectancy or the combined life expectancy of you and your spouse.

Your life expectancy? IRS mortality tables provide your life expectancy based on your age alone or your age and your spouse's (or beneficiary's) age together. The bank, mutual fund company, or brokerage that is the custodian of your IRA will calculate your IRA's required minimum distribution for you. Here's a general idea of how it works:

Divide your IRA account balance (that's the balance as of December 31 of last year) by your life expectancy. (See "Joint Life and Last Survivor Expectancy," pages 196–198, for a combined life expectancy of you and your spouse. For your single life expectancy, see the chart on page 181.) If your IRA was worth $40,000 by the time you reached age 70½ and your spouse age 76, for example, your

F.Y.I.

Thinking about withdrawing those IRA funds as soon as you can, without penalty? Consider your tax bracket first. If you are still working at age 59½ (the year when you may begin taking withdrawals without penalty), the money that you withdraw from your IRA will be taxed at the same rate as your salary. Those IRA withdrawals could even bump you into a higher tax bracket. Generally, you shouldn't withdraw funds from your IRA (if you can help it) until you are in a lower tax bracket.

Joint Life and Last Survivor Expectancy

Ages	50	51	52	53	54	55	56	57	58	59	60
45	42.0	41.6	41.3	41.0	40.7						
46	41.4	41.0	40.6	40.3	40.0						
47	40.8	40.4	40.0	39.7	39.3						
48	40.2	39.8	39.4	39.0	38.7						
49	39.7	39.3	38.8	38.4	38.1						
50	39.2	38.7	38.3	37.9	37.5						
51	38.7	38.2	37.8	37.3	36.9						
52	38.3	37.8	37.3	36.8	36.4						
53	37.9	37.3	36.8	36.3	35.8						
54	37.5	36.9	36.4	35.8	35.3						
55	37.1	36.5	35.9	35.4	34.9	34.4	33.9	33.5	33.1	32.7	32.3
56	36.8	36.1	35.6	35.0	34.4	33.9	33.4	33.0	32.5	32.1	31.7
57	36.4	35.8	35.2	34.6	34.0	33.5	33.0	32.5	32.0	31.6	31.2
58	36.1	35.5	34.8	34.2	33.6	33.1	32.5	32.0	31.5	31.1	30.6
59	35.9	35.2	34.5	33.9	33.3	32.7	32.1	31.6	31.1	30.6	30.1
60	35.6	34.9	34.2	33.6	32.9	32.3	31.7	31.2	30.6	30.1	29.7
61	35.4	34.6	33.9	33.3	32.6	32.0	31.4	30.8	30.2	29.7	29.2
62	35.1	34.4	33.7	33.0	32.3	31.7	31.0	30.4	29.9	29.3	28.8
63	34.9	34.2	33.5	32.7	32.0	31.4	30.7	30.1	29.5	28.9	28.4
64	34.8	34.0	33.2	32.5	31.8	31.1	30.4	29.8	29.2	28.6	28.0
65	34.6	33.8	33.0	32.3	31.6	30.9	30.2	29.5	28.9	28.2	27.6
66	34.4	33.6	32.9	32.1	31.4	30.6	29.9	29.2	28.6	27.9	27.3
67	34.3	33.5	32.7	31.9	31.2	30.4	29.7	29.0	28.3	27.6	27.0
68	34.2	33.4	32.5	31.8	31.0	30.2	29.5	28.8	28.1	27.4	26.7
69	34.1	33.2	32.4	31.6	30.8	30.1	29.3	28.6	27.8	27.1	26.5
70	34.0	33.1	32.3	31.5	30.7	29.9	29.1	28.4	27.6	26.9	26.2
71	33.9	33.0	32.2	31.4	30.5	29.7	29.0	28.2	27.5	26.7	26.0
72	33.8	32.9	32.1	31.2	30.4	29.6	28.8	28.1	27.3	26.5	25.8
73	33.7	32.8	32.0	31.1	30.3	29.5	28.7	27.9	27.1	26.4	25.6
74	33.6	32.8	31.9	31.1	30.2	29.4	28.6	27.8	27.0	26.2	25.5
75	33.6	32.7	31.8	31.0	30.1	29.3	28.5	27.7	26.9	26.1	25.3
76	33.5	32.6	31.8	30.9	30.1	29.2	28.4	27.6	26.8	26.0	25.2
77	33.5	32.6	31.7	30.8	30.0	29.1	28.3	27.5	26.7	25.9	25.1
78	33.4	32.5	31.7	30.8	29.9	29.1	28.2	27.4	26.6	25.8	25.0
79	33.4	32.5	31.6	30.7	29.9	29.0	28.2	27.3	26.5	25.7	24.9
80	33.4	32.5	31.6	30.7	29.8	29.0	28.1	27.3	26.4	25.6	24.8
81	33.3	32.4	31.5	30.7	29.8	28.9	28.1	27.2	26.4	25.5	24.7
82	33.3	32.4	31.5	30.6	29.7	28.9	28.0	27.2	26.3	25.5	24.6
83	33.3	32.4	31.5	30.6	29.7	28.8	28.0	27.1	26.3	25.4	24.6
84	33.2	32.3	31.4	30.6	29.7	28.8	27.9	27.1	26.2	25.4	24.5
85	33.2	32.3	31.4	30.5	29.6	28.8	27.9	27.0	26.2	25.3	24.5

Ages	61	62	63	64	65	66	67	68	69	70
45										
46										
47										
48										
49										
50										
51										
52										
53										
54										
55	32.0	31.7	31.4	31.1						
56	31.4	31.0	30.7	30.4						
57	30.8	30.4	30.1	29.8						
58	30.2	29.9	29.5	29.2						
59	29.7	29.3	28.9	28.6						
60	29.9	28.8	28.4	28.0						
61	28.7	28.3	27.8	27.4						
62	28.3	27.8	27.3	26.9						
63	27.8	27.3	26.9	26.4						
64	27.4	26.9	26.4	25.9						
65	27.1	26.5	26.0	25.5	25.0	24.6	24.2	23.8	23.4	23.1
66	26.7	26.1	25.6	25.1	24.6	24.1	23.7	23.3	22.9	22.5
67	26.4	25.8	25.2	24.7	24.2	23.7	23.2	22.8	22.4	22.0
68	26.1	25.5	24.9	24.3	23.8	23.3	22.8	22.3	21.9	21.5
69	25.8	25.2	24.6	24.0	23.4	22.9	22.4	21.9	21.5	21.1
70	25.6	24.9	24.3	23.7	23.1	22.5	22.0	21.5	21.1	20.6
71	25.3	24.7	24.0	23.4	22.8	22.2	21.7	21.2	20.7	20.2
72	25.1	24.4	23.8	23.1	22.5	21.9	21.3	20.8	20.3	19.8
73	24.9	24.2	23.5	22.9	22.2	21.6	21.0	20.5	20.0	19.4
74	24.7	24.0	23.3	22.7	22.0	21.4	20.8	20.2	19.6	19.1
75	24.6	23.8	23.1	22.4	21.8	21.1	20.5	19.9	19.3	18.8
76	24.4	23.7	23.0	22.3	21.6	20.9	20.3	19.7	19.1	18.5
77	24.3	23.6	22.8	22.1	21.4	20.7	20.1	19.4	18.8	18.3
78	24.2	23.4	22.7	21.9	21.2	20.5	19.9	19.2	18.6	18.0
79	24.1	23.3	22.6	21.8	21.1	20.4	19.7	19.0	18.4	17.8
80	24.0	23.2	22.4	21.7	21.0	20.2	19.5	18.9	18.2	17.6
81	23.9	23.1	22.3	21.6	20.8	20.1	19.4	18.7	18.1	17.4
82	23.8	23.0	22.3	21.5	20.7	20.0	19.3	18.6	17.9	17.3
83	23.8	23.0	22.2	21.4	20.6	19.9	19.2	18.5	17.8	17.1
84	23.7	22.9	22.1	21.3	20.5	19.8	19.1	18.4	17.7	17.0
85	23.7	22.8	22.0	21.3	20.5	19.7	19.0	18.3	17.6	16.9

Ages	71	72	73	74	75	76	77	78	79	80
45										
46										
47										
48										
49										
50										
51										
52										
53										
54										
55										
56										
57										
58										
59										
60										
61										
62										
63										
64										
65	22.8	22.5	22.2	22.0						
66	22.2	21.9	21.6	21.4						
67	21.7	21.3	21.0	20.8						
68	21.2	20.8	20.5	20.2						
69	20.7	20.3	20.0	19.6						
70	20.2	19.8	19.4	19.1						
71	19.8	19.4	19.0	18.6						
72	19.4	18.9	18.5	18.2						
73	19.0	18.5	18.1	17.7						
74	18.6	18.2	17.7	17.3						
75	18.3	17.8	17.3	16.9	16.5	16.1	15.8	15.4	15.1	14.9
76	18.0	17.5	17.0	16.5	16.1	15.7	15.4	15.0	14.7	14.4
77	17.7	17.2	16.7	16.2	15.8	15.4	15.0	14.6	14.3	14.0
78	17.5	16.9	16.4	15.9	15.4	15.0	14.6	14.2	13.9	13.5
79	17.2	16.7	16.1	15.6	15.1	14.7	14.3	13.9	13.5	13.2
80	17.0	16.4	15.9	15.4	14.9	14.4	14.0	13.5	13.2	12.8
81	16.8	16.2	15.7	15.1	14.6	14.1	13.7	13.2	12.8	12.5
82	16.6	16.0	15.5	14.9	14.4	13.9	13.4	13.0	12.5	12.2
83	16.5	15.9	15.3	14.7	14.2	13.7	13.2	12.7	12.3	11.9
84	16.3	15.7	15.1	14.5	14.0	13.5	13.0	12.5	12.0	11.6
85	16.2	15.6	15.0	14.4	13.8	13.3	12.8	12.3	11.8	11.4

Source: Internal Revenue Service, Publication 590.

required minimum distribution for the first year would be $2,222 ($40,000 divided by 18).

If you want your payments to be stretched out over a longer time period, figure your required minimum distribution based on the joint life expectancy of you and your spouse (or beneficiary).

You can withdraw the funds from your account in two basic ways:

1. **A lump-sum payout.** You can withdraw the entire balance of your IRA all at once. This means, of course, that you'll owe taxes on the entire balance all at once, too. Unfortunately, with an IRA you don't get the "forward averaging" tax break that you get if you take your 401(k) distribution in one lump sum. In some cases, you could end up giving half of your account balance to Uncle Sam.

2. **Periodic distributions.** You can take out whatever amount you want each year—and it can vary from year to year—as long as you meet the minimum distribution requirements. You can set up a more regulated withdrawal plan, too. IRA custodians will generally disburse checks as you request: monthly, quarterly, or semiannually. The advantage of this type of disbursement: While you enjoy a steady stream of income, your account is still growing tax-deferred.

Borrowing from Your IRA

Can you borrow money from your IRA? Strictly speaking, no. But you can transfer the money in your IRA to another IRA, once a year. (Perhaps you have your money invested in a stock mutual fund now and you want to move it to a different stock mutual fund.) What does this have to do with borrowing money from your IRA? When you transfer funds from one IRA to another, you are permitted to withdraw the funds yourself and to hold on to them for 60 days. (IRAs are not subject to the 20 percent mandatory withholding requirement that 401(k) distributions are.)

For those 60 days, you can do what you like with the money. You owe no taxes; you pay no penalties for the use of the money. You have, in effect, just received a short-term, interest-free loan. By the end of the 60 days, however, you must redeposit the funds into another IRA or you'll pay income taxes and possibly an early-withdrawal penalty on the funds.

Moving Your Traditional IRA Assets–After Retirement

Even if you're already taking your required minimum distributions from your IRA, you can still move your IRA assets from one investment to another if you like. Before you transfer funds, however, the IRS requires that you do one of the following:

1. Take your annual required distribution from your IRA.

2. Keep your annual required distribution with your previous custodian until you're ready to take that distribution this year, and transfer your other assets.

At this time, you can also still convert your traditional IRA to a Roth IRA if you like. But it's a two-step process. You can't simply move your assets from a traditional IRA held by one custodian to a Roth IRA held by another custodian. You must first convert your traditional IRA to a Roth IRA—either before or after you transfer the assets to a new custodian.

The Roth IRA

The new Roth IRA, which has been available since January of 1998, lets you save up to $2,000 per year into your account and is subject to many of the same rules that apply to a traditional IRA. Unlike a traditional IRA, however:

• You can't deduct contributions to a Roth IRA.

• If you satisfy the requirements, withdrawals from a Roth IRA are tax-free.

• You can continue to make contributions to your Roth IRA after you reach age 70½.

• There are no required distributions at any age. You can leave the money in your Roth IRA as long as you live.

• To qualify as a contributor to a Roth IRA, you must have income that falls within certain limits.

F.Y.I.

Only one IRA rollover is permitted per year. But if you transfer funds directly from one IRA custodian to another—and you don't receive the money yourself—this isn't considered a rollover. You may transfer your accounts as often as you like.

Contributions and Withdrawals Are Flexible

With a Roth IRA, there is no age limit for making contributions. You can keep making contributions to your Roth IRA as long as you have "earned" income, or compensation. (Earned income is the money that you receive from working, such as a salary or commission.)

Similarly, there is no requirement for making withdrawals during your retirement years. With a Roth IRA, you can leave your money in your account—untouched—for as long as you live. If you want, you can pass your Roth IRA assets to your beneficiaries. (This doesn't mean that your IRA will pass to your beneficiaries tax-free, however. The earnings will always be free from income taxes, of course, but in most situations your estate will pay estate taxes on your IRA assets.)

Taking Your Money Out– Before Retirement

If you began contributing to your Roth IRA at least five years ago, you won't incur a 10 percent early-withdrawal penalty if you take out the money before age 59½. Why? Because your Roth IRA contributions are made with after-tax dollars. That means you've already paid tax on the money, so you're allowed to withdraw those contributions at any time.

Your account earnings are different, however. You must pay income tax and an early-withdrawal penalty if:

• You withdraw the earnings in your Roth IRA before you reach age 59½

• You withdraw the earnings before you've met certain "aging" requirements. With a Roth IRA, you must leave your money invested for five years before you can withdraw the earnings tax-free. That five-year period generally begins on January 1 of the year that you made your first contribution or converted your traditional IRA to a Roth IRA.

Special "Hardship" Situations

If you're younger than age 59½, you can withdraw the earnings from your Roth IRA—without incurring a penalty—to help pay for the following financial hardships, as long as you've left your money in your account for at least five years:

• **First-time home purchase.** Over your lifetime, you can withdraw up to $10,000 to help you, your spouse, your children, even your grandchildren buy a first home. You won't pay any federal income tax on this withdrawal, either.

• **Higher education.** You can withdraw money to help yourself and those same family members pay for college or post-secondary education expenses such as tuition, books, supplies, and equipment.

• **Your death.** If you die before reaching age 59½, the assets in your Roth IRA will go to your beneficiary (or your estate) and will not be subject to the 10 percent early-withdrawal penalty. You won't pay any federal income tax on this withdrawal, either.

WHAT MATTERS, WHAT DOESN'T

What Matters
• You must pay a 10 percent penalty if you withdraw funds from a traditional IRA before you reach age 59½ unless you use the money for certain expenses.

• You can withdraw contributions made to your Roth IRA at any time, as long as it's been at least five years since you made your first contribution or converted your traditional IRA to a Roth IRA.

What Doesn't
• When withdrawing money from a Roth IRA, you needn't specify that withdrawals be taken from contributions. *All* withdrawals from a Roth IRA are taken first from contributions.

• Your child decides not to attend college. You can pay tax on the earnings in your Education IRA or roll it over to another child.

• **You become disabled.** If you become disabled before age 59½, any earnings that you withdraw from your Roth IRA won't be subject to a 10 percent early-withdrawal penalty. Disability, as defined by the IRS, means that "you cannot do any substantial gainful activity because of your physical or mental condition." A note from your physician outlining the length and degree of your disability is required. You won't pay any federal income tax on this withdrawal, either.

• **Payment of medical insurance premiums.** Even if you're under age 59½, you may not have to pay the 10 percent early-withdrawal penalty on the earnings in your account if you use the money withdrawn to pay for medical insurance for yourself, your spouse, and your dependents. The catch? You must have lost your job and received unemployment for more than 12 weeks.

• **Unreimbursed medical expenses.** You don't have to pay the 10 percent early-withdrawal penalty if you use the earnings withdrawn from your account to pay significant unreimbursed medical expenses. However, you can only take into account medical expenses that you would be able to deduct on your income taxes. In general, you can deduct only those unreimbursed expenses that exceed 7.5 percent of your adjusted gross income. (You don't have to itemize your deductions, however, to take advantage of this exception.)

• **Equal withdrawals made over a certain time period.** You can withdraw the earnings from your account penalty-free if you take the money as "a series of substantially equal payments" over your life expectancy or the joint life expectancy of you and your spouse. For the exception to apply, however, you must take at least one payment annually for at least five years, or until you reach age 59½ (whichever is the longer period).

The Education IRA

The Education IRA, which is a relatively new type of IRA, is not a retirement savings plan. It is a special IRA that helps families save money for their children's future college tuition and other school-related expenses such as books, supplies, and equipment.

You can't contribute more than $500 per year, per child. And if you earn too much money ($160,000 or more for a couple), you are not permitted to open this type of account.

Withdrawing the Funds

All contributions to an Education IRA are made for minors. You can open an account for your child, for example, as long as he or she is under 18 years of age. But you must stop making contributions to an Education IRA after your child has reached his or her 18th birthday.

Contributions made to an Education IRA are not tax-deductible. But the earnings aren't taxed if the money is used, upon withdrawal, for college tuition and related expenses.

Money invested in an Education IRA must be used by the time the child reaches age 30. (Actually, you have 30 days from the day your child turns age 30 to liquidate your account.) If your child de-

F.Y.I.

You can't take tax-free withdrawals from an Education IRA the same year that you use tax credits for college spending, such as the Hope Scholarship tax credit or the Lifetime Learning tax credit. Also, contributions to an Education IRA can't be made in the same year that you make state prepaid tuition plan payments for the same child.

F.Y.I.

You can contribute up to $500 per child, per year, to an Education IRA. That $500 contribution does not figure into your other IRA contributions, though. You can contribute $500 to an Education IRA and still contribute $2,000 to a traditional or Roth IRA.

cides not to attend a college, university, vocational school, or some other post-secondary school, you must withdraw the funds anyway and pay regular income taxes plus a 10 percent penalty on the earnings. You can easily get around this restriction by rolling over the unused money of one account into another child's (or grandchild's) Education IRA.

Generally, you can take withdrawals at any time—as long as you have expenses for post-secondary education. If, in any given year, your withdrawals exceed your expenses, you'll owe tax on the difference between expenses and the amount withdrawn.

Like the traditional IRA and the Roth IRA, an Education IRA lets you (or your estate, as the case may be) withdraw your funds—and not owe that 10 percent additional tax—if you become disabled or die.

Whether you're withdrawing funds from a traditional IRA, the newer, tax-free Roth IRA, or an Education IRA, there are certain rules limiting the withdrawal of your assets. When you reach age 70½, for example, you must begin taking the money out of a traditional IRA. With a Roth IRA, the money doesn't have to be withdrawn during your lifetime. Should you withdraw some or all of your assets prematurely, however, you'll generally owe taxes and penalties. Is it worth it? Only you can decide. In general, though, it's best to think of an IRA as its name implies: as an individual *retirement* account.

THE BOTTOM LINE

If you need cash, your IRA funds are accessible. You can withdraw funds from your account, penalty-free, for example, if you use the money to pay certain expenses, such as buying a first home. You can withdraw the contributions made to a Roth IRA—penalty-free—as long as you've met the five-year holding requirement. But bear in mind that your IRA is a *retirement savings* account. If you can, leave your IRA funds untouched—and still growing tax-deferred—until retirement.

Afterword

You have come a long way. Over the course of these nine chapters you've learned some important lessons about stocks and bonds, IRS regulations, and the ins and outs of 401(k) plans and individual retirement accounts. Most important, though, you've learned that you must take control of your own retirement savings.

For many of you that idea may have seemed downright intimidating at first. While it's true that Social Security benefits face an uncertain future and traditional pension plans are unrealistic for most employees in today's world of frequent career changes and downsizing, you aren't worried. Now you know that you can take charge of your financial future by planning and saving for your own retirement through an employer-sponsored 401(k) plan and/or an individual retirement account.

If your employer offers a 401(k) plan, it's best, in most cases, to take full advantage of that plan first. If your employer doesn't offer a 401(k) plan, if you're self-employed, or if you'd like to save additional funds for retirement, you should consider saving for your retirement with an IRA. Both of these plans are convenient, easy to use, and among the best retirement savings deals out there.

With a 401(k) plan, you contribute a portion of your salary, pre-tax, directly from your regular paychecks through automatic payroll deductions. (Saving this way is easy: You never see the money, so you don't miss it or have a chance to spend it elsewhere.) In many cases your employer will match a portion of your contributions. That's free money. If you don't contribute, though, you can't take advantage of the match.

What happens if you get fired, laid off, take early retirement, or simply switch jobs? No problem. Your 401(k) account is portable. It goes wherever you go. In many cases, you can simply roll the account over into another employer's 401(k) plan or you may move it into an IRA rollover. Either way, your money keeps growing tax-deferred.

Should you need to tap into those funds before retirement, in many cases, you can. Many 401(k) plans allow you to borrow up to half the money in your account (up to a $50,000 limit). The interest rates can be attractive with this type of loan, but borrowing will derail your retirement savings. If you qualify for a hardship withdrawal, you may be able to withdraw funds—penalty-free—before retirement.

With an individual retirement account, you can contribute up to $2,000 per year if you earn an income. Even if you don't work for pay, you may still be able to make "spousal" contributions. Depending upon your income and your ability to participate in an employer-sponsored retirement plan, you may be able to deduct your IRA contributions from your gross income.

Like a 401(k) plan, an IRA lets your money grow tax-deferred until you withdraw the funds at retirement. The new Roth IRA, however, lets you withdraw funds tax-free if you hold your account open for at least five years. You can also tap into your IRA before retirement to help you pay for certain financial hardships. But, like a premature withdrawal from a 401(k), you'll incur income taxes and penalties on an early withdrawal from your IRA account.

There are several different types of IRAs. The

traditional IRA, which is also referred to as an ordinary or regular IRA, lets you save up to $2,000 for retirement each year in a tax-deferred account. The new Roth IRA lets you avoid paying taxes on your earnings *forever*. A SIMPLE IRA allows small business owners to make IRA contributions for their employees. A SEP-IRA lets a self-employed worker contribute up to 15 percent of his or her income into a special IRA. And the new Education IRA lets you avoid paying taxes on savings for your children's college education. The amount that you can put into these accounts is limited to $500 per year, and you must meet certain income requirements to qualify.

Those are the facts. But, as you know, they only tell half the story. Once you understand how these retirement plans work—and how much money you're able to plunk into them—you must decide how the money will be invested. As a participant in a 401(k) plan or a holder of an IRA, you're responsible for making those investment decisions yourself.

To help make those decisions, you boned up on the basics of investing in Chapters 4 and 5. You learned about the different types of investments, such as stocks and bonds and various investment concepts like asset allocation and investment risk. You even learned about the different indices that can serve as benchmarks for your investments.

This is certainly a good start. You now should know enough to begin. But don't stop there. To become a savvy investor, you should read additional books and magazines on investing. Surf the Net. Visit the library. And, if need be, talk to a professional investment adviser.

In the final chapters you learned about withdrawing your money at retirement. Once you reach age 70½, you must begin to make minimum withdrawals from your 401(k) and your IRA. The new Roth IRA, however, isn't as restrictive. The money doesn't have to be withdrawn during your lifetime. Money invested in an Education IRA, however, must be used by the time the child reaches age 30, or rolled over into another child's Education IRA.

By the time you're ready to retire, you'll ideally have built up a sizeable nest egg. Whether you've saved and invested your money through a 401(k) plan, a traditional IRA, or the newer, tax-free Roth IRA, don't withdraw your funds too hastily. If you need to take money out to pay your living expenses (or to meet IRS requirements), do so. But use other sources of income that may be available to you, such as Social Security benefits or the money in a passbook savings account, *before* tapping into your retirement account. Why? The longer you keep your funds tucked away in a tax-deferred retirement account, the longer your money will keep on growing and compounding—*tax-deferred*. That means it'll be less likely that you'll outlive your money—and more likely that you'll have a comfortable retirement. Good luck, and enjoy.

Index

Books in the
Smart Guide™ series